Praise for *Storytelling for Grantseekers*

"Cheryl's unique approach, using storytelling to develop highly effective and competitive grants, is why I recommend her book to all my students."
—Vivienne French, part time faculty,
Truckee Meadows Community College, Reno, Nevada

"Cheryl Clarke breaks down the steps of writing a successful grant proposal and makes the entire process as natural as that of sharing the story of all the good work that our organizations do in the world. A must for both new and seasoned grantseekers."
—Dorotea Reyna, director of development,
California Institute of Integral Studies

"I eagerly await the new edition of *Storytelling for Grantseekers*. My first edition is worn out from good use."
—Jean Therrien, executive director,
Neighborhood Family Practice, Cleveland, Ohio

"Grantwriters looking for simple rules for writing a winning grant proposal should read Cheryl Clarke's book *Storytelling for Grantseekers*. Clarke's book is easy to read and follow, and her contention that grantmakers will be persuaded by a compelling story that demonstrates both knowledge of program and need for funding is spot-on."
—Catherine Fisher, trustee,
The Thomas J. Long Foundation

D0746315

Storytelling for Grantseekers

Storytelling for Grantseekers

A GUIDE TO CREATIVE
NONPROFIT FUNDRAISING

SECOND EDITION

Cheryl A. Clarke

Foreword by Frances N. Phillips

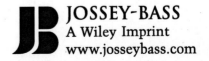

JOSSEY-BASS
A Wiley Imprint
www.josseybass.com

Published by Jossey-Bass
A Wiley Imprint
989 Market Street, San Francisco, CA 94103-1741—www.josseybass.com

Jossey-Bass books and products are available through most bookstores. To contact Jossey-Bass directly call our Customer Care Department within the U.S. at 800-956-7739, outside the U.S. at 317-572-3986, or fax 317-572-4002.

Jossey-Bass also publishes its books in a variety of electronic formats. Some content that appears in print may not be available in electronic books.

Library of Congress Cataloging-in-Publication Data

Clarke, Cheryl.
    Storytelling for grantseekers: a guide to creative nonprofit fundraising / Cheryl A. Clarke; foreword by Frances N. Phillips. —2nd ed.
        p.   cm.
    Includes index.
    ISBN 978-0-470-38122-9 (pbk.)
    1. Fund raising.   2. Proposal writing for grants.   I. Title.   II. Title: Storytelling for grantseekers.
    HV41.2.C53   2009
    658.15'224—dc22

                                                                    2008034933

10 9 8 7 6 5 4 3 2

C O N T E N T S

EXAMPLES

FOREWORD

In the early twentieth century, foundations set out to apply the rigors of science to solve society's problems. That is why I have long told grantwriting students that they would find the structure of a grant proposal familiar—similar to a basic scientific paper. It proposes a hypothesis (in its problem statement and objectives) and then outlines the methods that might be tested to achieve a result.

For nearly twenty years, I have been teaching grantwriting at San Francisco State University, and for years my students have looked muddled and sad upon hearing the science paper analogy. I remember finding evidence of their dismay in an e-mail from a talented student who was dropping the class because "the material was inherently dry." I found grantwriting fascinating, but I needed a new way to pass on my excitement.

Enter *Storytelling for Grantseekers*. In 2002 I was having lunch with a friend whose career had taken her back and forth "across the desk"—from working as a grantwriting consultant to working for a foundation and then back again to grantwriting. She told me about the first edition of *Storytelling for Grantseekers*. "It has revolutionized my grantwriting," she said. "I didn't think I could slog through another proposal, but I've really enjoyed the last two I wrote." On that recommendation, I hurried out and bought a copy, which I now use in my teaching.

Since reading that book, and now this second edition, I've come to appreciate that among the many fine books on grantwriting available, *Storytelling for Grantseekers* is distinctive in its goal to change our approach to the *writing*. While other texts may linger over the nuanced differences between objectives and outcomes or decode elaborate evaluation techniques, Clarke cheers her readers along as writers. I find her approach valuable—both for reluctant writers who need warm-up exercises and structured lessons to shove us beyond procrastination, and for seasoned grantwriters who get caught up in florid jargon of our fields and end up burying the main point. She asserts that a good proposal will convey a story—even if it is a proposal seeking support for a sophisticated bit of scientific research—and a good story is highly readable.

Though I worked for years in small nonprofits, I now spend the greater part of my work day as a senior program officer at a foundation. Some of the traits I value most in communicating with grantseekers are candor and honest self-reflection—nonprofits that tell the truth. One critical point to remember in heeding Clarke's advice to grantwriters is that we can enliven our writing by using the same techniques we would use in writing a good piece of fiction, but we should not fictionalize. An organization's truthfulness is essential to earning the trust of donors and foundations. Nevertheless, Clarke points out that a good proposal will feature heroes (and many, many nonprofits and their leaders are truly heroic), conflicts (the challenges of addressing society's most pressing problems), and inspiration (the visions those organizations maintain in their work).

If I were to sum up *Storytelling for Grantseekers*, I would say it is about the importance of readability. As a grantmaker, nearly every week I face stacks of proposals with varying degrees of readability. The good proposals make a clear point and substantiate it by putting their organization and ideas in context. They bring their characters to life—both leaders and constituents—and they enable me to recognize the value and meaning of their efforts. At the end of a good proposal, I am inspired. When I go to visit the organization and observe its work, I hope to find a clear correlation between the story they have told and the project I am observing.

My work is filled with good proposals and many that are less readable. Size and sophistication of a development department do not necessarily correlate with readability: some of the best ones have been written by volunteers. And while a project is not judged solely by the quality of the proposal writing, it is much easier for a program officer to work with and argue for a well-written document. As Clarke acknowledges, program officers' work often involves not only reviewing proposals, but also presenting arguments to other staff members and board members on behalf of the organizations submitting those proposals. The best thing a grantwriter can do is to arm foundation staff members with clear, honest, readable information so that they too can tell the organization's story—usually in a highly condensed form.

Storytelling for Grantseekers also walks its talk. Clarke's narrative is itself lively and highly readable. She provides examples illustrating her points and exercises to prime her readers' proposal writing. She also summarizes each chapter with a list of its key points, making it easy to follow the thread of the story she is telling us. And she answers the practical questions students and grantwriters always ask, such as, How long should this section be?

An air of mystery hovers around grantseeking—especially in the myth that only a handful of people have the inside track and know the tricks of the trade. It is true that decoding the preferences of foundations and striking up professional relationships with program officers and trustees comes with experience, but a good grant proposal in itself is not one bit mysterious. That's why I applaud the book you are about to read: it's not about the mystery or the science of grantwriting, but about the essence of good communications. Clarke has shaped a sophisticated yet highly readable volume, rich with examples, good humor, and stories.

September 2008

Frances N. Phillips
Instructor, Technical and Professional Writing,
San Francisco State University
and
Senior Program Officer,
The Walter and Elise Haas Fund

I dedicate this book to Richard, who steadied the
helm at home so I could focus on my writing; to Hannah,
who rocked the boat just enough to remind me of what's really important
in life; and to the memory of John and Lee for their dedication to
community service, which inspires me every day.

PREFACE

Storytelling is a powerful art form. Stories entertain, educate, and enlighten. They have the ability to transport an audience to another location and teach them about issues and people they may know nothing about. The same is true of grantwriting.

Yet many nonprofit and development professionals, both newcomers to the field and those with years of experience, contemplate the task of writing a grant proposal with as much enthusiasm as they would taking a trip to the dentist for a root canal. Those who are new to the field are likely to approach grantwriting with a "deer in the headlights" stare. The process seems daunting, intimidating, frightening. Those who have been in the nonprofit sector for a long time too often grudgingly accept grantwriting as a necessary chore, a boring task to complete in order to get to perhaps more enjoyable fundraising activities like soliciting major donors, drafting appeal letters, and organizing special events. For these folks, there is no joy in preparing a proposal; it is just something to get done, like making your bed and washing the dishes.

I have observed that only a rare few actually delight in seeking grants and writing grant proposals. I am one of these uncommon individuals. I wrote the first edition of this book to help my development colleagues get excited about the grantseeking area of fund development and to put the joy and creativity back into the grantseeking process. Considering the number of people who have contacted me after reading the first edition of my book, I think I succeeded. Dozens of times, I heard that *Storytelling for Grantseekers* inspired and informed grantwriters of all levels of experience. Better still, I heard from several who credit *Storytelling* with helping them secure a grant. There's no sweeter news than that!

When I was approached by my editor to work on a new edition of *Storytelling*, I didn't hesitate to agree. The book was ready for an update, though the message of *Storytelling* is still valid and will be a fresh concept for many in the nonprofit field.

The nonprofit field is dynamic, and technology is ever changing; I wanted an opportunity to acknowledge the changes and comment on them. Probably the most significant change in the grantseeking field over the past eight years is our use of the Internet. Today, we routinely use online technology to research funders, review and download guidelines, and submit proposals. In this second edition, I cover Internet issues in much greater depth than I did previously. Responding to reader requests, I also added new proposal excerpts from a wider range of nonprofit agencies (from grassroots groups to large institutions), and I included two full letter proposal examples in the Appendix. Finally, I reorganized a few chapters and added two new ones, and I tried to smooth out some rough grammatical spots.

I work in the nonprofit sector because it allows me to contribute in a meaningful way to my community. I suspect that the majority of you who read this book have chosen to work in the field for the same reason. It is our passion for the work, not the brass ring of stock options or growing retirement accounts, that keeps us going. Yet it is precisely this passion that is most often missing in grant proposals. My goal is to put the passion back in proposal writing!

I believe that you will be more enthusiastic about writing proposals, and your proposals will be more passionate and consequently more effective, when you begin using the storytelling technique described in this book. No doubt, this approach will be entirely new and different from the ones most of you are currently using.

For too many years, grantwriting workshops and how-to books have emphasized only the mechanics of writing grant proposals. For example, workshops and textbooks are good at covering such topics as the essential components of the proposal narrative; the definitions for outputs, process outcomes, impacts, goals, and objectives; and how to craft a program budget. But too many development professionals come away with glazed eyes after attending these workshops and reading such books. Grantwriters become overly concerned about technique and form. What's missing are the creativity and passion. That's what the storytelling approach puts back into the grantwriting process.

Whether you are a grantwriter, development director, executive director, board member, or volunteer, I hope you will come to the realization that grantseeking is as much a creative exercise as it is a technical one. By and large, grantwriters tell stories. There is great drama and excitement in our proposal stories. Telling a story is powerful. Writing a grant proposal is the telling of a powerful story.

CONTENT AND ORGANIZATION OF THIS BOOK

I begin with an introduction that discusses how the storytelling approach to grantseeking was developed and why you (and your agency) will benefit from using this method.

Yet before anyone sits down to write a proposal story, there are some preparatory steps to take. Chapter One describes what you and your agency should be doing to get ready for the grantseeking process. In Chapter Two, I offer guidance on how to effectively and efficiently research and identify your agency's target audience—that is, funders most likely to award a grant. This chapter also covers the broader topic of grantor-grantee relationships, from courtship and cultivation to stewardship.

Chapter Three is new. Although I covered letters of inquiry in the previous edition, the discussion was brief and somewhat buried. Because letters of inquiry are so widely used and often a critical "first step" in the grantseeking process, they deserve their own chapter.

Chapters Four through Seven demonstrate how to present your agency's story effectively in a proposal narrative. I believe that creative storytelling can be woven into the traditional proposal narrative form, as well as in online applications, and these chapters show you how this can be done. Chapter Four begins the sequence of chapters with a discussion of the importance of an opening "hook." From there, your story will progress to an introduction of the characters (the story's protagonist and other main characters) and the setting where your story takes place (location). In Chapter Five, I reveal what (not who) the antagonist is in our proposal stories and provide suggestions for fully developing this "character." In this part of your proposal stories, conflict is introduced and tensions mount. Chapter Six discusses the goals and objectives that will bring a full or partial resolution to the conflict. The evaluation and future funding sections in a proposal can be considered your story's epilogue and sequel; these sections are covered in Chapter Seven.

Proposal stories are not just told in words. Chapter Eight explains how to translate your agency's narrative story into the language of numbers in an accompanying proposal budget.

Once the full proposal story is written, it must be "marketed." In Chapter Nine, I cover the marketing elements of a proposal, namely the summary, titles, and headings. Chapter Ten follows with a discussion of the proper "packaging" of a grant proposal, including what attachments to enclose and what delivery method to use.

Because our proposal stories are often transformed to "live theater," I added a new chapter (Chapter Eleven) devoted to site visits and to the communications we have with funders while our proposals are pending and after a decision has been made. Finally, Chapter Twelve (also new) addresses the topic of how grant-writing skills are transferable to other fundraising areas and even outside the nonprofit field.

Whenever possible, I have included examples from actual grant proposals to illustrate the concepts presented in this book. These proposal excerpts are the works of several excellent writers, who are credited in the text for their work, and myself. In some circumstances, agency names have been changed to respect the wishes of the agency.

In the course of writing this book, what I have learned by rereading my own grant proposals is that I have not yet written the absolutely perfect proposal. And I believe that my talented colleagues would agree that they have yet to write one either. Has anyone drafted the perfect proposal? Has any author ever written the perfect book? I am pleased when I have come close to approaching perfection, and with every proposal I write, I continue to strive for that ideal.

I wrote this book because I have an interesting, compelling story to tell. I hope that in reading this book, you will see that you do too. I wish all readers happy, successful grantseeking!

September 2008

Cheryl A. Clarke
Mill Valley, California

ACKNOWLEDGMENTS

The very best stories succeed because the action is propelled forward by strong, intelligent, and charismatic characters. I was extremely fortunate to have just such a wonderful cast to assist me in making this book a reality, and, therefore, I have several people to thank.

First Edition

Marian Breeze saw the potential and gave me unflagging encouragement during the writing of the first edition and the editing of the second. Initially, Marian was going to play a much larger role in the creation of this book; however, motherhood intervened, and she needed to direct her energies to caring for her family. Still, Marian faithfully read my drafts during this busy period in her life when she had precious little extra time. She generously provided thoughtful comments and asked insightful questions. I am deeply indebted to Marian and thank her for sharing her knowledge of the nonprofit field, offering her well-honed editing skills, and, most of all, having a delightful sense of humor.

I also thank Guy Biederman, my fiction writing instructor. Under Guy's tutelage, I learned much about the craft of writing good short stories, and I apply this knowledge when preparing grant proposals. When I was first toying with the idea of this book, I spoke with Guy about the important role storytelling has played throughout civilization. Our conversation helped convince me that I really did have a story to tell.

Mary Gregory and Dorotea Reyna read and critiqued early drafts of my manuscript, and I thank these dear friends and colleagues for the time they spent doing so. They will see that I incorporated many of their helpful suggestions in the final product.

I deeply appreciate and thank each of the nonprofit agencies that gave me permission to reprint portions of their grant proposals in this book. I also acknowledge my inspiring colleagues who generously shared their proposal narratives with me. They are Marta Johnson and Roberta Swan (Philanthropy By Design), Nora Hirschler, MD (Blood Centers of the Pacific), Rochelle Nason (League to Save Lake Tahoe), Clifford Janoff (Bay Area Ridge Trail Council), Barbara Brenner (Breast Cancer Action), and fundraising consultants Susan Fox, Nancy Quinn, and Laura McCrea. My special thanks also go to Cindy Rasicot and Jo Wegeforth for ceaselessly providing me with good cheer along the way.

Polishing a draft into a final manuscript can be an arduous task. I thank editor Johanna Vondeling for her gentle persuasion and generous support.

Lastly, I thank the "breakfast bunch"—Laura McCrea, Lee Follett, and Pamela Cook—for patiently enduring a year of my almost total devotion to this project. The fact that we continued to eat blueberry pancakes together is proof that the best friendships can survive the writing of a book.

Second Edition

A new edition means I have some new people to acknowledge and thank. At the top of the list is Susan Fox, my colleague, coauthor, and friend. I appreciate her wisdom and wit, her encouragement and support.

Once again, my colleagues (and the agencies they work for) came through for me, answering my call for new proposal examples and excerpts. In fact, I had so many responses that not all were able to make the "final cut." Yet all are deeply thanked: Marie Beichert (Ella Baker Center for Human Rights), Toni Doyle, Carol Lena Figueiredo (New Door Ventures), Susan Fox (St. Francis Center and Lion's Center for the Visually Impaired of Diablo Valley), Judy Kunofsky (Petaluma Bounty and The Other Bar), William Masterson (California Society of Jesus), Yvonne Prouse (Jesuit Volunteer Corps), Eleanor Smith, Jennifer Yeagley (LightHouse for the Blind and Visually Impaired and Child Advocates San Antonio).

I had the good fortune once again to work with a talented editor, Allison Brunner, whose energy and enthusiasm brightened my days at the computer.

Finally, I thank all my clients over the years: your work is inspirational, and I am grateful to have had the opportunity to craft your proposal stories.

THE AUTHOR

Cheryl A. Clarke is an accomplished grantwriter and storyteller. Based in the San Francisco Bay Area, Cheryl is a fundraising consultant, trainer, and speaker who has helped hundreds of nonprofit organizations raise money in awarded grants and philanthropic contributions. She is also an award-winning writer of short fiction.

A self-described "recovering lawyer," Cheryl graduated from Northwestern University with a bachelor of science degree in journalism, and received her law degree from the University of San Francisco School of Law. While practicing law, she joined the board of directors of a nonprofit organization and discovered her real career passion. Within a year, she had made a successful career transition and was appointed the director of development and alumni relations at the University of San Francisco School of Law. She has also held fundraising positions at the University of California–San Francisco and The Marine Mammal Center. She is a member of the Association of Fundraising Professionals and Development Executives Roundtable.

With Susan Fox, Cheryl coauthored *Grant Proposal Makeover: Transform Your Request from No to Yes* (Jossey-Bass, 2007) and is a contributing author of *Team-Based Fundraising Step by Step* (Jossey-Bass, 2000). Her short stories have been published in several literary magazines.

In addition to writing, Cheryl enjoys teaching. She conducts webinars and workshops on fundraising techniques, board development, and grantwriting. She is a much sought-after keynote speaker and presenter, having presented workshops at several local and international conferences of the Association of Fundraising Professionals and the national conference of the American Association of Grant Professionals.

Introduction
Why Storytelling?

From the beginning of time, people have communicated their ideas, values, and lessons through stories. At first, stories were told in the oral tradition, often over an evening fire, and passed along from generation to generation. Some stories were later depicted through pictures drawn on cave walls or carved into stone. Over time, our ancestors developed written forms of language and began to memorialize their stories in writing.

The power of both true and fictional stories is demonstrated throughout history and literature. For example, in the Bible, Jesus uses parables—narrative short stories—to convey a double, or metaphorical, meaning. In the Greek tradition, fables and myths are impossible fictional stories that communicate a deeper, again metaphorical, message. *Beowulf* and *The Canterbury Tales* are early epic tales that provide fictionalized accounts of historical (or at least partially historical) events.

Regarding the significance of storytelling throughout the history of humankind, Joel Orosz, author of *The Insider's Guide to Grantmaking* (Jossey-Bass, 2000), says, "In history, great leaders aren't necessarily the smarter people; they're just the ones who tell the best stories" (personal communication, 2001).

People always have used stories to inform, instruct, and persuade others. And storytelling is very much alive today. In fact, a Google search of the word "storytelling" yielded more than fifteen million hits.

Storytelling is used effectively in both the for-profit and nonprofit fields. In the business world, stories are often used in advertisements to sell everything from instant coffee to athletic shoes to weight-loss programs. In the nonprofit field, executive directors and development directors rely on storytelling techniques to recruit volunteers, appeal to potential donors, and inform and influence the broader community. So it makes sense to use this powerful technique when seeking grants. Yet I realized that nobody else in the grantwriting field was talking about integrating storytelling methods into grantseeking. This void convinced me that I had a story to tell to the nonprofit world. This is the story told in this book.

I consciously began integrating the storytelling technique into my grantseeking activities in general, and into my grant proposals in particular, more than a decade ago. There are three good reasons why I started doing so.

First, one of my personal pursuits is writing short fiction. I came to realize that strong grantwriting uses most, if not all, of the same elements that are found in good fiction. Accordingly, the storytelling techniques I developed while working on my short fiction naturally started finding their way into my grant proposals.

Second, I believe that storytelling is at the core of all successful fundraising. Storytelling is an effective way to communicate a need, offer a solution, and present an opportunity for someone to help by making a financial contribution. Appeal letters, Web sites, telethons, and major-donor campaigns use storytelling techniques to inform and motivate potential donors. Shouldn't grant proposals do the same?

Third, I listened to what grantmakers themselves were advising applicants to do. What I heard foundation program officers and others who review proposals say was "Tell us your story." As the saying goes, "Everyone loves a good story," and this includes program officers.

Joel Orosz offers the following observation (personal communication, 2001): "When Charles Dickens wanted to talk about generosity, he wrote *A Christmas Carol*, not a grant proposal. Ultimately, the grantseeker has a story to tell in the proposal. Rather than disguise or hide it, why not just tell it?"

The former chair of an employee contributions committee whose corporation annually donates more than a quarter of a million dollars to charities in the San Francisco Bay Area echoes Orosz's advice: "We'd love to see more proposals presented as stories. Those that do are easier to read and understand, and they are the ones that are more apt to be funded."

So the best news for grantseekers is this: using the storytelling technique works!

WHAT IS THE STORYTELLING METHOD?

Nearly every story ever written or told has certain common elements. These elements include characters (usually both a protagonist and an antagonist, as well as assorted other major and minor characters), a setting (both time and place), and a plot. In a typical story plotline, the author first introduces the characters, then creates a conflict between the characters and builds tension. Most likely, the tension escalates to a climactic or pivotal moment, when something happens that forever changes one or more of the lead characters. After this dramatic event, the story eases to its conclusion.

A strong, effective proposal narrative has these same elements: characters, a setting, and a plot that includes the building of tension, the drama of a climactic moment, and the resolution offered by a satisfying conclusion. This book will explain how these story line elements actually fit within the standard narrative structure of a proposal and how you can begin to incorporate them into your own grant proposals.

And as you probably already know, there is more to successful grantseeking than simply writing a proposal. Identifying which funders you should submit your proposals to, developing a relationship with these grantmakers, and effectively presenting your proposal package are all part of the grantseeking process. The storytelling technique applies to each and every step along the way.

YOU ARE ALREADY A STORYTELLER

I want to emphasize that you do not need to be an accomplished fiction writer to use the storytelling method presented in this book. Whether you realize it or not, you are already a storyteller. In our daily lives, the oral tradition of storytelling is very much alive and well. "What's new with you?" asks a friend or colleague. And you proceed to talk about what's been going on in your life. That's a story, and you're telling it.

In your professional life you are a storyteller when, at either a work or social gathering, you answer questions such as these: What does your nonprofit agency do? What's its mission? What kinds of people does your agency help? What's the biggest problem facing your agency these days? How much money does it take to run the agency? What does your agency plan to accomplish in the coming year? Most likely, not a day goes by that you don't have an occasion to tell somebody at least a portion of your agency's story.

Although you may feel comfortable verbally discussing your agency's story, perhaps it hasn't been as easy to actually write it down in the form of a grant proposal. I'll show you how to get your agency's story on paper so that your proposals will be not only more fun to write but also more enjoyable for the funder to read. You'll learn how to grab the reader's attention with the opening sentence and hold it until the closing paragraph.

There's another reason why the storytelling technique should be a comfortable one to master. Throughout our lives, we all not only tell stories to each other but also read and listen to stories as well. We all know a good story when we read one, whether it is short fiction or a novel the length of *War and Peace*. It is the book you just can't bear to set down or the chapter you must finish before going to bed. When you feel this way, you know that the writer has done a good job of capturing your attention. That's the kind of mesmerizing drama and excitement I want you to create for those funders reading and reviewing your grant proposals. Let's get started!

First Steps
Getting Ready for Grantseeking

chapter
ONE

A s any writer will tell you, a lot of preparation usually takes place before any words are actually written. This is also true for grantseekers. First comes the idea, the inspiration. For storytellers, ideas are sparked in their rich imaginations. With nonprofit agencies, ideas can be generated by a variety of people working for or with the agency. Most frequently, it is the executive director or program director who initially conceives an idea for a new program or project that will need new funding in order to be implemented. Or the plan may be simply to keep an existing program going. In either case, the nonprofit agency needs money, and it is decided (generally by the executive director or development director) that approaching grantmakers is a good strategy for securing the necessary funding. But before you or anyone else in your agency begins to draft a grant proposal, additional steps must be taken.

GET PREPARED

It is not unusual for storytellers, and specifically writers, to conduct extensive research before they begin to draft their stories. Some retreat to the library, where they read everything they can about a particular topic. Others try to get

5

firsthand experience. Authors have been known to take flying lessons, spend a season working on a fishing vessel, or volunteer at a dude ranch in order to prepare for writing their stories.

Grantwriters should be equally prepared. Before attempting to write a proposal, learn as much about your agency as you possibly can. True, we all get busy and overcommitted in our work and daily lives, but spending a day out in the field is priceless. Observe or experience your agency's work firsthand. Talk to the clients your agency helps. Spend a day shadowing your agency's program director, social worker, artistic director, or education coordinator. I guarantee that you will soak up more information than you ever would by visiting your agency's Web site or reading your agency's annual report. Nothing substitutes for being in the field—nothing.

IS THE PROJECT FUNDABLE?

After a program idea has been formulated, the next step is to assess whether the proposed program or project is fundable. The reality is that not all ideas will germinate into fundable programs or projects. It's a bit of a jungle out there in the grantseeking world. Only the fittest survive. So how does an agency determine whether a proposed program or project is likely to be funded? Consider the following questions:

- Is the program or project compatible with the agency's central mission or purpose? (I've seen too many nonprofit agencies chase potential grant dollars by developing programs that were not aligned with their core mission simply to apply for available grant funding. This is letting the tail wag the dog. Do not be tempted to do that. Rather, create only programs that further your agency's mission. Then seek grant funding for those programs. Be assured that if your agency's work serves a critical need, there are foundations and corporations out there willing to provide funds.)

- Does your agency have the expertise and staff resources to carry out the program?

- Can your agency manage the proposed expansion of services?

- Is the proposed program distinguishable from other similar programs in the community? If so, what specific niche will this program or project fill?

- If other agencies are doing similar work, has your agency explored opportunities for collaboration?

- Is there internal support from the board of directors and senior staff for the proposed program?

If your agency can answer yes to each of these questions, then it is well on its way to developing a fundable program. If any answer is no, then perhaps your agency is heading down the wrong path—a road not likely to lead to grant funding.

For example, if your agency does not have the necessary staff expertise to launch a new initiative, it should not pursue grant funding until it has addressed this issue. Consider what could be done to acquire people with the necessary experience and qualifications. This may mean increasing the new program's budget, thereby enabling the agency to hire the additional staff needed. Or it may mean recruiting unpaid volunteers who can be trained to do the work. Another possible alternative is for the agency to explore collaborating with another nonprofit organization that has the appropriate staff expertise.

The point I want to make is that nonprofit agencies are most likely to secure grants when they develop fundable programs. From ideas spring new programs, new initiatives, and these can be bold and inventive, yet they must also present the likelihood of success. If a program seems doomed to failure from its inception, no funder is likely to want to invest in it.

DON'T LET A BAD PROPOSAL DISGUISE A GOOD IDEA

Our challenge is to present to potential funders the most persuasive, creative, and well-written grant proposals that describe the very best programs and initiatives—that is, the ones most likely to succeed in efficiently and effectively delivering valuable services to agency clients. Unfortunately, just as some literary rubbish ends up in the bookstores (and even on the best-sellers list), bad proposals describing bad ideas arrive in the in-boxes of foundation program officers every single day. A veteran program officer, much like a seasoned literary agent, has seen it all—from the very best to the very worst. In fact, most program officers can classify a proposal into one of four basic categories, as Joel Orosz does in his book *The Insider's Guide to Grantmaking* (Jossey-Bass, 2000).

First, there's the bad idea–bad proposal, which is a deadly combination. It's the proposal that presents an idea that is ill conceived, underdeveloped, or just plain unworkable. The proposal isn't even well written, making it all the easier for the program officer to toss the submission into the reject pile. These are easy ones for the program officer to dispense with.

The second type of proposal is the devious bad idea–good proposal. Narratives like this are often the products of professional grantwriters, masters of the fine art of spinning golden words. Masquerading under slick, sophisticated writing lurks a really bad or weak program idea. But with a smoothly crafted proposal, it's harder to recognize it. Yet don't kid yourself—the vast majority of program officers are going to see right through the veil of crafty wordplay. A proposal that falls into this category is not likely to get funded either.

More frustrating are submissions that fall into the good idea–bad proposal category. With these proposals, the gem of an idea truly worthy of funding lies buried under disorganized, sloppy, or terrible writing. Most program officers are willing to make the journey and try to find the treasure, provided they see a flicker of a good, or even brilliant, idea. Sadly, a few won't bother, and thus some truly wonderful programs or projects won't get funded.

Proposal submissions in the final category are of course a joy to behold and read. These are the ones that present a well-developed idea by telling a good story. These are the "10s," the ones that get four stars, the ones that should win the Pulitzer Prize. It should be no surprise that these are the grant proposals that have the best chance of being funded. In a philanthropic environment where the ratio of submitted to funded proposals is often ten to one or twelve to one (with some funders it can even be as daunting as twenty to one), excellence is what you should be striving for.

IS YOUR STORY READY TO BE TOLD?

Not all stories are ready to be told. Grantwriters have to know when they have a compelling, urgent story to tell and when there are serious loose ends to tidy up before pen should be put to paper (or, in today's nonprofit office, before the computer should be turned on). I am talking about those unusual circumstances when the grantseeking process (and, for that matter, possibly all fundraising activities) should be temporarily halted. For in a nonprofit agency's life, there may be times when it is prudent to stop fundraising until the crisis has passed.

What times are these? Whenever the agency's credibility is in doubt and its ability to do its work is called into question. For example, the following situations may require a pause in grantseeking:

- When there is extremely high turnover on the board of directors
- When a seriously difficult executive director transition is occurring
- When the agency has been rocked by public scandal or has received extremely negative press
- When there is inadequate staff to plan and implement the program for which funding is sought

In each of the situations just described (or other such extenuating circumstances that merit a temporary suspension of fundraising activities, including grantseeking), the agency needs to get its house in order before fundraising can proceed. There is a simple reason for this. When making funding decisions, grantmakers look for agencies that are fiscally stable, that demonstrate competence and the ability to do good, solid work, that have steady internal leadership (for example, from the board of directors and chief executive officer), that are respected in the community, and that are trustworthy. Agencies experiencing one or more of the challenges just listed are therefore at an extreme disadvantage when seeking grant funding. Other agencies without these troubling issues present a stronger case for support. And although it is precisely during such trying times that a nonprofit agency is most likely to be in need of contributed dollars, asking for grant support is likely to be frustrating or even futile, and it may even jeopardize future opportunities for funding.

To be successful at grantseeking, you must tell your agency's story from a position of organizational strength.

KNOW WHAT YOU'RE RAISING MONEY FOR

In grantseeking, as with all fundraising activities, it is critical for anyone working on a proposal to know specifically what the agency is raising money for. The financial needs of a nonprofit agency fall into six broad categories. So far, I have referred to only one of those six, which is program or project support. (Note that a *project* is a task—something of limited duration—whereas a *program* is something likely to continue indefinitely.) The other five categories of financial needs are the following:

- *Funds for capital or equipment purchases.* This is so-called bricks-and-sticks or bricks-and-mortar funding, which includes funding for things like building or renovating facilities, acquiring raw land, or purchasing large pieces of equipment, such as vehicles, computers, telephone systems, or medical testing devices.

- *Endowment funds.* Think of these as an agency's piggy bank. They're like savings or retirement accounts. Money is prudently invested, and the interest earned is used to support the agency's programs, projects, and general operations.

- *Funds for technical development or capacity building.* Such funds help an agency gain expertise that will enable it to move to the next level. This includes, for example, management, financial, and fundraising training.

- *Seed funding.* These are funds for brand-new start-up agencies. This is crucial incubation money that helps an agency get established.

- *General operating funds.* These are funds that cannot otherwise be placed in a program or project budget and that cover all of an agency's day-to-day expenses, such as salaries, rent, insurance, and supplies.

Grantmakers frequently limit their funding to one or two specific financial needs. A great number fund new or continuing programs or projects. Other foundations award grants only for capital projects. Some prefer to assist fledgling organizations by providing seed funding. A significant number help nonprofits, frequently those they already support with program or operating grants, from the inside by giving technical assistance and capacity-building grants. A few make gifts to establish or increase endowments. And finally, there are those cherished foundations that make unrestricted grants, which can be used to support an agency's general operations.

Be aware that your agency is likely to have multiple financial needs at any given time. Certainly, every nonprofit agency has an ongoing need for general operating support in order to pay its basic bills and to make its payroll. The vast majority of nonprofit agencies will also need funds to support services and programs. From time to time, many agencies will have capital or equipment needs. Matching the right funder with your agency's specific financial needs is extremely important and is discussed more fully in Chapter Two.

The fact that every nonprofit I know needs funding is not surprising. The fact that some nonprofits don't have a clear understanding of what they need funding *for* is. I occasionally get phone calls that go something like this:

EXECUTIVE DIRECTOR: Hi. I'm calling because we need a grant.
ME: For what?
EXECUTIVE DIRECTOR: Money.
ME: For what?
EXECUTIVE DIRECTOR: Money.

You get the point. Executive directors and nonprofit staff generally know they need funding, but they can't always articulate what they need the funds for. And if they can't express the need to you or me, we won't be able to do a very good job telling a prospective funder. When approaching grantmakers, it is essential that we clearly state what the grant, if awarded, will fund.

GET READY TO TELL YOUR STORY

If your agency has a fundable idea to present to potential grantmakers, then the next question to address is whether you are well prepared and personally ready to tell your agency's story.

No matter whether you're an old-timer or a brand-new employee, you should not begin to write a grant proposal until you are adequately prepared. And all grantseekers are better prepared if they know as much as possible about the nonprofit agency they work for and the field the agency works in (such as education, social justice, health care, or the visual arts). As previously noted, I recommend that from time to time you get out of your office to see and experience the actual work your agency does. You may have worked for the same organization for several years, perhaps having held several different positions in the agency, and may already be very knowledgeable. Or you may be new to your agency and perhaps even to the nonprofit sector. If that is the case, preparing a grant proposal is a great way for you to become well acquainted with your agency and the field in general.

This is one of the things I love most about grantwriting: you get to wear many hats! In addition to writer, you are also a reporter and a researcher.

Be a Reporter

To tell your agency's story effectively, you first need information, and to get information, you must often play the role of reporter. In this capacity, you will frequently find it necessary and appropriate to interview various staff members at your agency, such as the program director, finance director, personnel director, and executive director. Armed with a reporter's notepad, you must get the specifics from these individuals before you can begin to prepare a grant proposal.

For example, suppose that you are a grantwriter working for a nonprofit blood bank in a major urban area; the blood bank is having difficulty recruiting blood donors from the city's largest ethnic population. The blood bank's executive director thinks that to increase blood donations, it would be a good idea for the center to hire an outreach coordinator who can focus recruitment efforts on this ethnic community. The executive director hopes this program will be funded through grants from foundations in the community and asks you to draft the proposal. As a resourceful reporter, what do you need to do?

Well, you'd probably want to begin by interviewing the head of donor recruitment at the blood bank, especially because the proposed outreach coordinator would report to her. You would want to know why it is important for the blood bank to increase blood donations from this ethnic group. Are there cultural barriers that prevent people in this ethnic community from giving blood? You would also want to learn what vision the head of donor recruitment has for the proposed program. With whom in the ethnic community would the outreach coordinator forge relationships, and how? What kinds of written and online recruitment materials may need to be developed? Would these materials need to be translated into another language? How and to whom would such materials be distributed?

These are the types of questions that can best be answered by interviewing agency staff in your role as reporter.

When talking with staff, don't forget those folks in the finance department. You'll need to work with them on the budget that will accompany the proposal. In some situations, the finance department will prepare the budget, which you will then need to review carefully. In others, you will work closely with the finance department in building a budget together. A full discussion of budgets is found in Chapter Eight.

If you worked at the blood center, you would likely first talk with either the center's finance director or the personnel director in order to determine a salary range for the new outreach coordinator and other related program expenses.

In addition to interviewing agency personnel, you might also find it worthwhile to talk with one or more clients of your agency, especially if you are gathering quotes or testimonials. Often there is no substitute for words spoken from the heart by people who have been helped by your agency. As discussed in Chapter Five, client quotes become the rich dialogue in your proposal story.

Be a Researcher

In addition to functioning as an ace reporter, you also get an opportunity to be a crackerjack researcher. Key facts and figures that will strengthen your case for support do not fall from the sky. Sometimes they are provided to you by a program director or can be found in agency documents (such as prior evaluation reports), but often you must do independent research to find the data you'll need to write a strong proposal. To be an effective and efficient researcher, you should become familiar with online resources that are relevant to your agency's field of work. U.S. Census, county, local government, and chamber of commerce Web sites are good places to start. Googling relevant key words will frequently lead you to other helpful sources.

Returning to our blood bank example, your proposal narrative would be even more persuasive if it included statistics to show the low percentage of blood donations from the targeted ethnic population. Therefore, you may need to do some independent research if this information is not readily available from internal sources at the blood bank. Perhaps your agency's case would be further enhanced if you were able to frame it within a broader geographic context, demonstrating that this is a statewide or even national issue. Additional research may reveal how other blood centers around the country have dealt with the challenge of recruiting more blood donors from specific ethnic groups.

As you can see, being a grantwriter is not one-dimensional. At any given time, you may be a writer, an intrepid reporter, or a thorough researcher. The job of grantwriting will certainly keep you busy!

"TALK" YOUR STORY

As I've already said, I believe that each of us is a competent storyteller. Telling stories is an integral part of our daily lives. And yet telling an agency's story in a grant proposal can seem so daunting. Why? One of the obvious reasons is that most of our daily storytelling is verbal. Frequently, it is the act of writing the story down that freezes us. So how can you take the spoken word and get it written down?

First, turn off that editor's voice in your head. Too often we believe that the written word needs to be more formal or perfect than the way we speak. We begin to write, yet find ourselves saying, "That doesn't sound right." So we stop. We delete. We labor over the same sentence for hours.

May I make a suggestion? To use a popular slogan: just do it. Just write. I call it the "dirty draft." It isn't pretty, but it gets the job done. I put words and thoughts on paper. I write quickly, not pausing to parse every word or mull over each phrase. Sometimes I leave blanks or mark where I want to find a more descriptive or precise word. Sooner rather than later, I have a first draft. Once I do, I can go back and edit, revise, and move copy around, polishing my rough draft into a smooth gem. And that's so much easier than facing the terror of a blank page.

Second, aim to write the way you speak rather than the way you think you should write. We know what we want to say, but too often we feel the overwhelming need to write in a formal, frequently stilted, manner. We choose big words instead of short ones because we believe that they make us sound smarter. We write long, complex sentences for the same reason. In doing so, we run the risk of losing clarity. In my experience, writing more like the way we speak helps keep proposal narratives clear, concise, and to the point. And they will read as if written by a passionate human being rather than a computer thesaurus.

If you still have trouble getting started, try thinking about why you chose to work for this particular agency and about the clients it serves, the work it does, and the difference it makes in the life of the community. Write down your thoughts, your answers. You may be surprised by how passionate you are about the cause, and this is most likely to be conveyed on paper. This is a terrific warm-up exercise before beginning to draft that otherwise daunting proposal.

I suggest that once you have a draft that you are satisfied with, put it aside for several days. Then go back over the copy one more time. Does the proposal answer the questions asked by the funder? Does it flow like a well-written story? Is it well organized? Does the narrative contain drama and excitement? Does it grab the reader's attention with the first sentence and hold it throughout? Until you can answer yes to each of these questions, you have more work to do.

Always make certain that you give yourself enough time to edit and revise. I cannot emphasize this point enough. The preparation (research and fact gathering) that goes into getting ready to write a proposal takes time. The actual writing of a grant proposal takes time. Usually lots of time. Successful grant proposals typically are not prepared in a few hours, days, or even a week. Schedule

Time to Write!

This is a book about writing. It's time for you to do just that, so take out a pen or turn on your computer. This is an exercise I frequently use to open my grantwriting workshops.

I like adjectives and adverbs. By definition, they are descriptive words that give color and texture to our writing. Like seasonings, a few well-chosen words will come together to create a delicious dish (or nicely crafted proposal). Use too many, and you ruin the soup. I like using adjectives and adverbs in grant proposals because they force us to be precise with language.

Here's what I want you to do:

- Using only five to seven adverbs and adjectives, describe your agency.
- No nouns, pronouns, verbs, or articles are allowed.
- You may not use the adjectives "unique" and "innovative." (Every nonprofit agency can lay claim to those descriptors, and they have therefore lost their meaning.)

Think it can't be done? What type of nonprofit organization am I describing with these few carefully chosen words?

- Historical
- Archival
- Educational
- Local
- Kid-friendly
- Acclaimed

What do you think this agency is? (See the footnote at the end of the chapter for the answer.)

Now it is your turn. Time to start flexing that writing muscle.

sufficient time to research and gather information, then schedule even more time to write and revise. In the best-case scenario, allow yourself at least three to four weeks for the whole process.

I've received many calls from frantic executive directors and development professionals asking for help in preparing a grant proposal when the submission deadline is only days away. Under such constraints, there isn't enough time to do the job right. Sadly, I have to turn them down. I won't be able to do a good job, and they won't be satisfied with the outcome when they hear from the grant-maker. So my advice is to plan ahead and give yourself sufficient time for any unexpected delays or problems.

SUMMARY

As anyone who has ever painted a room knows, at least 80 percent of the job is in the preparation. The same can be said for grantseeking, as well as for all fund-raising activities. Success is achieved through adequate preparation. Here are the key points on grantseeking preparation that have been covered in this chapter:

- Spend time out of your office and in the field in order to witness firsthand the programs and services offered by your nonprofit agency and to meet the clients being served.

- Determine whether new ideas for programs and projects are fundable.

- Understand what specifically you're raising money for.

- Assume the roles of reporter and researcher when gathering information to be included in a proposal.

- Consider *talking* instead of *writing* your story.

Time to Write! answer: a county history museum

Research and Relationships

Finding and Cultivating Your Audience

Authors of children's literature don't want their books sitting on the shelves of a bookstore's sci-fi section, and sci-fi writers would be unhappy to find their stories plunked down in the middle of the romance section. That's because storytellers, and in this case authors, want to reach their primary audience: that segment of the population most likely to purchase and read their works. So writers of children's fiction want their titles placed in the children's literature section, and sci-fi writers are happiest when their creative works are located with other books of the same genre.

The notion that writers (not to mention their publishers) want to get their books in front of the right audience translates beautifully to the grantseeking field. To have the best chance of securing all-important grant funding, you must get your agency's grant proposals before the right audience—that is, those grantmakers most likely to fund your project or program. Yet identifying the right audience of potential funders isn't as easy and straightforward as it is for those who write children's literature, science fiction, mystery novels, romance novels, and the like. Therefore, this chapter discusses how to find and cultivate the best audience of grantmakers for your nonprofit agency.

EFFICIENT RESEARCH: THE FOUR FILTERS PLUS ONE

At the time of the writing of this edition, there are close to one hundred thousand foundations in the United States, and that number is expected to grow steadily in the years ahead. There are also hundreds of thousands of corporations and businesses operating nationwide, many of which have grantmaking programs. In addition, there are countless government agencies (city, county, state, and federal) that make grants.

Given the sheer number of potential grantmakers, how does one efficiently and effectively research and identify the best possible prospects? Research can too often seem like the black hole of fundraising, a bottomless pit that development professionals fall into and can't get out of. It can seem like a daunting and perhaps overwhelming task—unless you have a system for conducting your research.

To streamline your research and make it an efficient, less time-consuming process, I recommend using the "four-filters-plus-one method." By using this method, you will be able to quickly assess whether a grantmaker is a good fit for your agency and to filter out all others.

The first four filters, or criteria, I use to determine whether a foundation, corporation, or government agency is a true prospect for grant funding are the following: subject area, geographic preference, type of financial need, and the typical dollar range of grants awarded. This information is generally readily available in the various foundation and corporate directories (both electronic and hard copy) and may be used to guide your online searches. (Where to go to conduct your research comes a little later in the chapter.) The fifth criterion, or the plus-one filter as I like to call it, is different from the other four because it is not readily apparent from a review of foundation and corporate summaries. The fifth filter involves relationships, those personal connections between your nonprofit agency and a potential grantmaker.

A tip for making research more efficient: review the first two criteria (subject matter and geography) before going any further. If you identify a funder that supports agencies doing the work that yours does, but sets geographic restrictions on its grantmaking, and your agency doesn't fit within the geographic boundaries, then Stop! Don't read another word. You're only wasting your time by reading about a funder that does not fund in your area or does not fund the type of work that your agency does. I'll have a little more to say about this as we go on.

THE FOUR FILTERS PLUS ONE—UP CLOSE

Let's take a closer look at each of these filters, or screening criteria, to see how they can be used to determine whether or not a potential grantmaker is likely to be a good fit.

Subject Area

It should almost go without saying that one of the most important filters is subject area, which describes the field in which an agency conducts its work. Is your agency working in the arena of health care, the arts, social services, social justice, education, the environment, or something else? Funders frequently prioritize their grantmaking by subject area, which will be noted in their guidelines and then reported in the many available grantmaker directories.

Seek to identify those funders with whom your nonprofit agency has an alignment of interest. Accordingly, if you work for an agency dealing with the mental health of seniors, then you should be looking for grantmakers that list mental health, seniors, or both as among their funding priorities. Similarly, conservation groups get matched with environmental funders, schools are best teamed with grantmakers that fund education, a dance group should seek out funders of the performing arts, and so on.

On occasion, I've had nonprofit professionals ask me whether they should approach a funder that doesn't already award grants in their field. Their thinking is that perhaps something different will appeal to the funder. I discourage this approach. It is better to find a match based on similar subject area, because we are grantseekers, not missionaries. We shouldn't try to convert a foundation that has expressed a preference for funding in a given area. Doing so is likely to be a waste of time.

For example, a family foundation that expressly states that it supports the performing arts is not a good prospect for an agency concerned with the mental health of seniors. Approaching this funder on behalf of a senior citizen mental health initiative will be a colossal waste of time and energy. This grantmaker, presumably after thoughtful consideration, analysis, and deliberation, has chosen the subject area it will concentrate on funding (in this case, the performing arts). Consequently, your lobbying efforts are likely to have little effect. Yet I nevertheless hear nonprofit organizations (generally those with little experience in grantseeking) emphatically state that they are going to approach a particular foundation precisely because the foundation has never before funded in their field. And they are determined to convince that foundation to make an exception. In such situations, all I can do is wish these zealots the best.

Geographic Preference

The next filter, or screening device, is the expressed geographic preference of the funder. In fact, coupled with subject area, these are the two most important filters. Why? In order for a grantmaker to be a legitimate potential investor in your agency, it must make grants in the geographic region where your agency does its work. Suppose you identify a foundation that seems to be a perfect subject-matter fit with your agency. However, this funder restricts its grantmaking activities to a small geographic area that is two thousand miles away, or perhaps just two hundred miles, from where your agency is located. Is there any reason to approach this funder? The answer is no. This grantmaker is not a good geographic fit with your agency.

What this means is that a Los Angeles–based agency addressing the mental health needs of senior citizens should be looking for grantmakers that (1) identify mental health, seniors, or both as a funding priority and (2) make grants in the city of Los Angeles. A foundation which indicates that senior health programs are a funding priority but restricts its funding to the San Francisco Bay Area will be of little help to that Los Angeles–based agency.

Remember that geographic location is of the utmost importance to corporate and business grantmakers. Corporations prefer to fund, and frequently will only fund, in those communities where they are headquartered or have major facilities. The reason for this should be obvious. Companies choose to fund the work of nonprofit agencies in communities where their employees and primary customers reside. They want to support nonprofit agencies where their employees are volunteering or serving on boards of directors. Businesses seek to address local problems or unmet needs that most directly affect the communities where their employees and customers live, work, and play.

You may know that Widgets International is the largest company in the United States and that its annual grantmaking program annually awards billions of dollars in grants. However, if in researching Widgets International you discover that the company makes these grants only in its headquarters city of Lucky Falls, Montana, then you should move on to the next potential grantmaker (unless your agency is lucky enough to be located in Lucky Falls). No matter how large, how generous, or how publicly visible a corporation (or any other grantmaker) is, if it doesn't make grants in the geographic region served by your agency, it's time to move on.

Given the sheer number of grantmakers nationwide, it is crucial to review them as quickly as possible when conducting your initial research, eliminating those funders that are not likely to support your agency. In my experience, I'm able to screen out all but the best prospects by using the twin filters of subject area and geographic preference first.

Type of Financial Need

After you have reviewed potential grantmakers on the basis of subject matter and geography, the next filter I suggest you use is the type of financial need. Once you've identified a grantmaker that funds your agency's subject area and awards grants in your geographic region, see whether the grantmaker funds the type of financial need you're seeking funding for.

In Chapter One, I discussed how you need to know what you are fundraising for in order to present a compelling story. I noted that there are six broad categories of financial needs, including the need for (1) funds to support a program or project, (2) funds for capital or equipment purchases, (3) endowment funds, (4) funds for technical development or capacity building, (5) seed funding, and (6) general operating funds.

It should come as no surprise that grantmakers often specify the precise types of financial needs they will support. And they often get even more specific than the six broad categories mentioned. Here's a partial sampling of the range of financial needs grantmakers may be willing to support: annual campaigns, documentary films, conferences and workshops, building renovations, acquisitions of real property, fundraising events, raffles, scientific research, scholarships, and stipends.

Given the breadth of supported financial needs, you may wonder whether there's anything some grantmaker out there won't fund. Yes, there is one thing—a deficit. If your agency has overspent its financial resources and its balance sheet is awash in a sea of red ink, don't count on a foundation, corporation, or government agency to bail out your organization. Grantmakers don't provide funding to cover deficits. The reasoning is straightforward: running a deficit is a strong indication that a nonprofit agency lacks fiscal prudence and sound financial judgment, and that it may lack the ability to sustain its programs in the future.

This goes to the heart of agency credibility. When there's a deficit, the agency does not look credible. A prospective funder has good reason to question whether the financially troubled agency will manage the spending of new grant funds any better than it has its monetary resources in the past. When evaluated alongside other grant applicants that can demonstrate sound fiscal management, an agency that cannot balance its books does not stack up well.

This is not to say that nonprofit agencies, just like for-profit businesses, don't from time to time find themselves having financial or cash flow problems. Perhaps the arrival of government grant funds has been delayed, or the agency's roof has unexpectedly started leaking and a new one must be put on, or the agency's rent has skyrocketed. As we all know, not every contingency can be planned for. However, it is precisely for these contingencies that prudent nonprofit agencies set aside some money. They create a cash reserve, a sum of money that can be drawn on when these things happen. These types of rare occurrences, when reasonably explained to potential grantmakers, may excuse a weak balance sheet or a modest operating deficit. But usually only once. Funders want to invest in financially stable organizations, not those in precarious financial shape.

Dollar Range of Grants

The last of the four filters is the dollar range of grants typically made by the potential funder. Why is this important or even necessary to know? Because as grantseekers, we try to match grantmaker capacity with agency need.

For example, let's suppose you are seeking grant support for a multimillion-dollar capital campaign, and you identify a foundation that meets each of the three criteria previously discussed (subject area, geographic area, and type of financial support) but awards grants only in the $500 to $1,000 range. At the beginning stage of a multimillion-dollar capital campaign, you need to secure six- and seven-figure gifts; therefore, you wouldn't put this foundation on your "A list" of potential supporters. Rather, you shouldn't consider approaching this foundation until much later in the campaign, after your agency has already secured its large leadership gifts.

Here's another example on a much smaller scale. Suppose you work for a small, grassroots organization that needs $2,500 for a new project it hopes to launch. You identify a foundation that meets each of the previously described filters; however, this funder makes huge grants, say in the range of $100,000 to $500,000. Your request is probably much too small. This foundation has the capacity to award—and the history of awarding—large, six-figure grants to support large, complex programs and projects. This foundation does not want to review requests for tiny grants, regardless of the proposed program's merit. Instead, consider funders that award smaller, or mini, grants to secure the needed $2,500.

Grant range counts. But be careful when you look at the average grant—as opposed to the range of grants—awarded by a potential funder. Focusing only on the average grant size can mislead you. For any given period of time, this number can be skewed, particularly if the grantmaker recently has awarded an especially large grant. For example, consider a foundation that typically awards grants in the $30,000 to $50,000 range. This funder's average grant size will be artificially high if it has just made an unusual million-dollar award. Looking at only the average grant size for the time period in question, you may incorrectly conclude that the foundation routinely makes six-figure grants. Examining a funder's typical grant range will usually give you the best indication as to whether your request for funds is a proper fit.

Relationships: The Plus-One Filter

The final criterion you should use in determining whether a funder is a good fit for your agency, the plus-one filter, concerns relationships, those personal connections between your agency and the grantmaker. Compared with the first four filters, which can each be applied based on readily available information in the ample resource materials on grantmakers (such as foundation and corporate directories and databases), the plus-one filter is more difficult to apply. Uncovering relationships that exist between your agency and a potential grantmaker requires a bit more effort. True, foundation and corporate directories and databases, along with funder Web sites, annual reports, and guidelines, will almost always identify their officers and trustees. But what you still don't know is whether these people have any linkages to anyone connected with your agency. Finding out if they do requires two steps.

First, whenever you uncover a potential bona fide grantmaker (that is, one that meets the four qualifying criteria), you should make a list of that funder's officers and directors. After you've done this, the second step is to circulate this list among the key people associated with your agency. Most notably, this means your agency's board of directors, although you should also not overlook other key volunteers and staff members, for they know people too. See if anyone affiliated with your agency recognizes the names of the potential funder's officers and trustees. Better still, find out if anyone has an actual connection to these people.

Many board members profess to be "not well connected." I've heard this many times from several different clients. But it's just not true. The reality is that everyone knows somebody, and not surprisingly, board members sometimes know people affiliated with grantmakers in the community.

One of my favorite stories on this subject concerns a fledgling nonprofit organization that was operating on a shoestring budget of less than $100,000 per year; it was governed by a small board of directors and managed by a part-time office administrator. To jump-start this agency's grantseeking efforts, I conducted some initial research and developed a list of about a dozen potential funders. I then prepared a list of the officers and trustees affiliated with these possible funders and took it to a board meeting for review. Before the group even looked at the list, several members voiced the usual protests about not knowing anyone. With a little of my cajoling, they finally agreed to review the list. And what happened? The chair of the board suddenly exclaimed that she not only knew the president of one of the listed foundations but that he was also her neighbor! Hallelujah! A connection, a linkage, was uncovered. The postscript to this story is that after a few conversations between the board chair and the foundation president, the agency was invited to submit a proposal and was ultimately awarded a $10,000 grant!

I can't guarantee a satisfactory outcome like this every time; however, you won't know what relationships exist between your agency and a possible grantmaker unless you inquire. Developing a list of foundation officers and trustees is a good place to start.

HOW MUCH MONEY TO REQUEST

Executive directors and development directors often ask how much money they should request from a particular funder. Suppose that a community foundation normally makes grants in the $5,000 to $50,000 range. Should a first-time applicant request a safe $5,000 or "go for broke" and ask for $50,000? To properly answer this question, it is important to keep in mind that first-time applicants are trying to establish a relationship with a new funder. And you should be aware that the first grant is the hardest money to get from a grantmaker. Therefore, my general rule of thumb is not to be too aggressive with a first-time proposal submission. Ask for an amount somewhere in the middle of the range. It may even be a wise strategy to go in a little lower. Once your agency has an established relationship with a grantmaker, it is easier to engage in a dialogue with that funder about increasing the amount requested in a renewal application.

Having told you my strategy for determining the appropriate amount to ask, I am honor bound to report that I once worked with an executive director who takes a dramatically different approach. He always asked for the highest grant award possible, hoping to catch the "big one"—and he was successful some of the time. Although he didn't always get many grants, those he did secure were often big. Would he have been more successful in terms of quantity if he had asked funders for a more modest sum? It is impossible to say. But what this illustrates is that seeking and securing grants is an art, not a hard science. As this book attempts to demonstrate, certain grantseeking techniques and methods work better than others. Yet there are points in the whole grantseeking process where the best you can do is follow your inner voice, your intuition. Mine tends to lean toward a more conservative approach, whereas this executive director follows a more aggressive path. And neither of us is completely right or wrong.

HOW LONG YOUR GRANTMAKER LIST SHOULD BE

Like a miner panning for gold, a grantseeker uses the four-filters-plus-one method to find the golden nuggets, those funders that are most likely to fund your agency and its work. How many potential funders will you be able to identify? The short answer is: it depends.

How many bona fide grantmakers you will uncover depends on many factors, such as where your agency is located, how long it has been in existence, and whether the subject matter is currently popular with funders. Certainly, nonprofit agencies in large urban areas will have more possibilities than agencies in less-populated rural communities. Well-established agencies, those that have been serving their communities for several years, are also likely to have a longer list of possibilities simply because they know the funders and the funders know them. Lastly, it is a reality that grantmaker interest in specific causes waxes and wanes over time. If a particular cause or area of interest has the attention of the funding community at a given time, then agencies working in that field will probably find more potential supporters.

I advise nonprofit agencies to look for quality, not quantity, when researching potential funders. A list of "only" six or seven strong potential grantmakers is fine. A list of one or two dozen names is even better. Be cautious if you end up with a significantly longer list than that. If you do, you're probably not stringently screening prospects with the four filters, and you may not be filtering out enough unlikely prospects. Chasing after long shots will not only lower your success rate but will also soak up valuable time and energy. Most nonprofit professionals, and this includes executive directors, development directors, and program staff, already carry a full plate of work. Be careful about how much more you add to that pile. Strive for efficiency when doing your grant research because this will lead to grantseeking effectiveness.

HOW TO FIND THE GRANTMAKERS

In the first part of this chapter, I provided you with a process for conducting your funder research. Now I want to give you some suggestions on where you can go to undertake your research endeavors.

The Foundation Center Libraries

If you are fortunate enough to work in close proximity to one of the five resource centers operated by the Foundation Center, run, don't walk, to the nearest one! Currently, the Foundation Center houses its national collections in New York City and Washington DC and has field operations in Atlanta, Cleveland, and San Francisco. At each of these resource centers, grantseekers have free access to the center's own publications and resources (including its excellent grantmaker directories and electronic databases), as well as to thousands of books, periodicals, and other research materials related to foundation and corporate giving. The Foundation Center also has a very helpful Web site (the address at the time of this writing is www.fdncenter.org).

If you don't live or work close to a Foundation Center library, don't despair; the Foundation Center also works with a network of nearly four hundred cooperating libraries nationwide. These libraries, which include nonprofit resource centers, public libraries, and community foundation libraries, offer grantseekers most, if not all, of the basic research materials you'll need.

The Internet

I joined the nonprofit field before the dawn of the Internet era, back when I used to traipse to a library to pour through thick reference guides to do funder research. The Internet has dramatically changed the way we conduct our research by putting much of the information we'll ever need just a keystroke away. More and more grantmakers, be they foundations or corporations, have Web sites that contain guidelines, annual reports, and lists of prior grantees. If you have a funder in mind or know its Web address, you can easily get to this online information. A greater challenge is to identify new bona fide potential funders by searching the Web.

It takes skill and patience to craft a good search. You can use Boolean criteria (AND/OR) for searches on the four filters we've discussed. For example, you can search for funders of a specific subject area in a particular geographic region. Or you can search for funders that support certain types of needs (for example, capital, general operating, scholarships) for certain types of causes (social justice, arts, education, health care, and so on).

My personal preference is to begin by using Foundation Center reference databases and developing an initial list of potential funders. I then visit the Web sites of every funder on the list, provided it has a Web site. (A number of grant-makers, even the smaller family foundations, have learned that a Web site will save them the time and expense of having to respond to telephone inquiries or letters requesting guidelines and deadline information.) At this point, I try to expand my universe of potential donors by undertaking a broader Internet search. I know that I am using appropriate search words if the funders I've previously identified come up in the search.

Nonprofit Agencies Doing Similar Work

Other nonprofit agencies in the field that are doing work similar to your agency's are a wonderful but frequently overlooked resource. Why are they a good resource? Presumably, these nonprofit organizations receive funding from grant-makers that fund in a particular field of interest. Therefore, it is probable that these funders would be interested in also funding your agency.

How can you find out who is funding these other agencies? Review their donor lists! This is public, published information, often readily available on the agency Web site, in agency newsletters, annual reports, and other publications. Many nonprofit agencies, especially museums, theaters, schools, hospitals, and others whose physical sites include public spaces; also acknowledge their major donors with donor walls, plaques, and the like. Do you notice these when you visit? You should, because you can bet that many of your colleagues are paying attention to what foundations and corporations are funding your agency!

On this subject I have a humorous story to share. It's about an ingenious donor researcher working in the development office of a major public university. A new building had recently been completed and dedicated at his school's cross-town rival, a prestigious private college. The researcher wanted to make certain that he was up-to-date on his knowledge of which grantmakers were funding capital projects for higher education. So he took a "field trip" across town to visit the new building and was duly impressed by the dignified donor wall located in the lobby. But there were so many names that he feared he'd be there all day jotting them down. So this clever development professional took out a camera! He snapped a roll of film, had the film processed, and had the photos enlarged so he could read the funder names. I still admire his genius.

Publications and Other Media

Nonprofit periodicals, local newspapers, and, more rarely, the electronic media are other possible sources for information about who's funding whom. Try to read, or at least scan, as many relevant publications as is reasonably possible. For-profit businesses are especially interested in seeing that their good deeds get publicity. Thus it is not unusual for a newspaper, particularly a neighborhood paper or one in a smaller community, to run a "grip and grin" photo. You know—the one where a corporate representative is presenting an oversize check to a local charity. In recent years, some newspapers have added a nonprofit section as a regular feature. Society columns, besides providing gossip fodder, are another place where good deeds, which include corporate as well as individual largesse, are recognized. So read, read, read!

Your Professional Network

Another often overlooked resource are our friends, relatives, and professional colleagues. People, especially those working in or with the nonprofit field, can be a great source of information. By nature, most fundraising professionals are extroverted folk, and we enjoy getting together with colleagues at professional meetings, conferences, workshops, and symposia. But whether you're an extrovert or an introvert, the fact remains that a lot of useful information circulates at these events, and unless you're there, you won't hear it. So make certain that you attend those appropriate professional and community functions. If you do, don't be surprised if you hear a tidbit like this: "Say, did you hear that the Children's Sports Institute just got a $75,000 grant from the Community Foundation?"

RECRUITING OTHERS TO HELP YOU

By now you might be wondering if it is really possible for one person to do all the work that goes into researching potential grantmakers. If you don't think so, well, you're absolutely right. It's really not possible for any single individual to do it all.

You need to do what you can, what is humanly possible. I recommend that you recruit others to assist you in the search for potential grantmakers for your agency in order to expand your capabilities and reach. Each person who is closely connected to your nonprofit agency—whether on the staff, on the board of directors, or working as a volunteer—can also serve as the agency's eyes and ears. Engage these folks in the research process. Encourage them to read other nonprofit agency newsletters and annual reports, scan the local papers, watch the evening news, attend various community events, and listen to what others in the community are saying about funding opportunities. If you are the professional grantseeker at your agency, suggest that they report back to you whenever there's a "hot tip" about a new potential funding source. As an intrepid reporter (remember how you play that role when ferreting out background information for preparing a proposal?), once you have a lead, you can take over and do whatever further research is needed.

I can hardly overemphasize the following point: the process of grantseeking, including funder research, is an ongoing one. You cannot complete the research task in an afternoon or even a full day. The grantmaking environment is simply too big and too fluid. New foundations are continually being established. Existing ones change their giving priorities. New corporations move into the area. Old businesses close or leave. Government funding allocations change as new policies are created and laws are adopted. In this ever-changing, dynamic funder universe, there's always new information to acquire and assimilate. That's why grantseeking, and especially funder research, is a year-round activity.

WHAT TO DO WITH YOUR "SHORT LIST" OF GRANTMAKERS

For nonprofit agencies that are just beginning to seek grants, the objective is to develop a realistic and manageable list of potential grantmakers. As I've already noted, a list of one hundred or more names is probably neither. A more useful list will probably be composed of a dozen or two names. Please keep in mind that this is just to give you a rough idea of what you're striving to develop. If you uncover thirty-five honest-to-goodness prospective funders, that's terrific. And if you identify only six grantmakers, that's okay too. It's not the quantity as much as it is the quality that matters. You want to find the best possible, most likely grant-funding sources that you can.

If you work for an established agency that has been in existence for several decades, then you probably already have a core list of grant funders. These will include current supporters, as well as those foundations, corporations, and government agencies that have funded the agency in the recent past. Your objective in this case is to add new names to this pool of grantmakers. Through your research efforts, it may be realistic to identify only one, two, or perhaps half a dozen potential new funders. Once again, it's not a numbers game in which the highest score wins. Rather, success in grantseeking is built on the quality of the prospects.

Regardless of whether you are working for a brand-new start-up organization or a well-established community institution, once you have a "starter list" of the most likely grantmakers, the following steps come next:

1. *Obtain the funder's most current guidelines and grant application.* In today's Internet age, this is easier than ever. A great number of foundations and corporations—probably the majority—now have a Web presence, which means you can visit a funder's Web site to view guidelines and download an application. For an ever-increasing number of funders, you may be able or even required to apply online.

2. *Read and review the funder's guidelines carefully.* As most of us know, the devil's always in the details. Nowhere is this truer than in grantseeking, and particularly when you are trying to figure out all the technical requirements that need to be fulfilled in order to get a grant proposal submitted. There's the all-important deadline. And if you are submitting by mail, you need to know whether this means a postmark date or the date of actual receipt of the proposal by the funder.

Electronic submissions frequently require strict attention to space limitations and formatting requirements; with paper submissions, you must be concerned about limitations on the length of the proposal, what type size to use, how many copies to enclose, what attachments to include, and so on. Generally, all your questions about such matters have been considered by the grantmaker and are answered in the guidelines—if only they are read! So read carefully.

If after reading the guidelines you are still in doubt about a particular detail, what should you do? First, if possible, contact the funder by either e-mail or telephone to clarify your understanding. If you are unable to reach the funder (remember that small family foundations often do not have any staff members to respond to these requests), then you'll have to rely on your own good judgment.

3. *Review the funder's most recent IRS Form 990.* The 990 is the informational tax return that all nonprofits (including foundations) are required to file annually with the IRS. This is a public document, and the Internet has enabled 990s to be posted and easily accessible (for example, at the Guidestar Web site at www.guidestar.com). The 990 provides a wealth of information about a funder, including its total assets (in dollars), the total amount distributed, a complete list of grantees and awarded amounts, and a list of trustees or directors. Reviewing this information will help yield a more complete profile of the grantmaker you want to approach for funding.

4. *Prepare a yearlong grants calendar.* The grantseeking process is a year-round activity. Given all the responsibilities of a grantwriter and to help make sense of what otherwise could be chaos, I strongly recommend creating a grants calendar, which you can put on a spreadsheet relatively easily. A grants calendar doesn't have to be fancy, but it should be a useful tool that keeps you mindful of upcoming proposal deadlines and the status of your agency's grantseeking activities.

At minimum, a grants calendar should list which funders your agency plans to submit proposals to, the amount of each request, and the specific program or project for which you are seeking funding. I've also found it useful to include a place for additional comments, especially regarding the status of the submission. Often, I also add a column to list the funder's trustees and officers and to note any personal relationships between the funder and agency, as well as a column to indicate the priority ranking of the prospects ("A's" being those I will apply to first; followed by B's, which will be approached only after all of the A's have received proposals; and finally the C's, who are the last to be approached). Exhibit 2.1 shows a format for a basic grants calendar.

Cultivating an Audience

You have a list of prospects organized in a grants calendar—now what? Before you start writing, I suggest that you or someone else from your agency familiar with the request (such as the program director who will manage the program) call the funder if at all possible. Some funders readily encourage, or even require, phone calls from would-be applicants. If that's the case, consider this an opportunity to

Exhibit 2.1.
Sample Grants Calendar Format

Name of Foundation	Fundable Program or Project	Dollar Amount of Request	Submission Deadline	Proposal Status and Comments

tell your story in the oral tradition. Be well prepared. Have close at hand all the information you may need so that you can easily refer to any key facts and figures. Be ready to answer questions. Listen carefully to what the program officer has to say. These conversations can help shape your request and guide you through the application process.

Keep in mind that not every funder welcomes phone calls and not every program officer returns calls. If you find that after leaving three or four messages you haven't heard back, then it is probably safe to conclude that you aren't going to. You'll have to proceed without the benefit of advice from a real person at the funder's office.

Time to Write!

This chapter has focused on researching, not writing. But because this is a book principally about writing, it's time for you to do just that, though admittedly this isn't the most creative of assignments. If your organization does not yet have a grants calendar, I want you to create one right now.

Using Connections

Earlier in the chapter, I noted that identifying any personal relationships existing between your agency and a funder is important. Sometimes they are essential, as in those situations where a foundation does not accept unsolicited proposals. Most likely, you'll need a personal connection with the funder in order to be invited to submit your request. Don't waste your time without one, or your proposal will just end up in the circular file.

When personal relationships exist, they are frequently between one of your board members and a trustee at a foundation. Such connections are golden and should be treated as such. For example, a board member with linkages to a foundation may be able to facilitate an introductory meeting or telephone call between your executive director and a foundation program officer. Or, by talking with a foundation trustee, your board member may be able to gain valuable insight into the foundation's current funding preferences and obtain tips for how you can best present your request. Or the board member may serve as a valuable advocate in championing your agency's case for support to the decision makers at the foundation. These are all examples of how a personal connection can be positive and helpful.

Yet there are pitfalls to watch out for. The most serious is allowing a personal relationship to circumvent the funder's established procedures. Guard against this. Program officers have a job to do, and they must follow internal procedures that direct how proposals are reviewed and funding decisions are made. These procedures must be respected.

Accordingly, if a board member from your agency knows a foundation trustee, it is not advisable to approach the trustee with your proposal and bypass the program officer. Rather, it is a better practice to honor procedure by being transparent about any personal connection between agency and foundation. In your cover letter, mention the board member's relationship to the trustee, and copy the trustee. If you have an opportunity to speak directly with the program officer, be candid about disclosing this relationship. Keeping all parties informed is always the best policy.

There's a downside to not doing so. When personal relationships are used to secure grant funding, program officers are being sidestepped, and their authority is undermined. Under such circumstances, a program officer is certain to be upset, and rightly so. This is not the kind of impression your agency wants to make with a program officer, especially one who will be monitoring your agency for the duration of the grant period. It could make for a long and uncomfortable year. Furthermore, a program officer may remain with a foundation long after a trustee has left. You may be dealing with the program officer for many, many years. Or the program officer may leave one foundation and take a position with another, carrying negative feelings with him. Under either scenario, wouldn't you rather have a friend?

BUSTING A POPULAR MYTH

Sometimes the adage is true: it's not what you know but who you know.

Having said this, one of the biggest myths in grantseeking is that you *must* know somebody in order to get funding. This simply isn't true. Every day, non-profit agencies receive grant funding from grantmakers without having the benefit of an inside connection. These agencies are funded because they are credible, they provide valuable services to meet community needs, and their proposals present a strong case for support.

For the majority of agencies, the submission of a proposal or letter of inquiry is the first step toward developing a relationship with a grantmaker. This is especially true in large urban areas, where thousands of nonprofits compete for limited grant funding. With time and staffing in short supply, grantmakers are unable to become familiar with all potential grant applicants. In many instances, a funder will first hear of an agency only when that nonprofit approaches the funder for a grant. In contrast, it is not unusual for grantmakers and grantseekers to be very well acquainted with each other in smaller towns and cities.

SUMMARY

Delivering your compelling story to the right audience of potential funders is essential in successful grantseeking. This chapter discussed how to identify the best funders for your agency and how to cultivate that relationship once identified. Key suggestions included the following:

- Use the four filters plus one (subject area, geographic preference, type of financial need, dollar range of grants, and personal relationships) to screen out all but the most likely funders for your agency.

- Be thorough in conducting your research, using such resources as the Foundation Center library, community foundation libraries, public libraries, the Internet, other nonprofit agencies doing similar work, newspapers and other publications, and your professional network.

- Recruit those persons affiliated with your agency—staff, board, and volunteers—to assist you in the process.
- Keep in mind that identifying your potential audience is a year-round activity.
- Remember: you don't always need to know someone to get a grant.
- Recognize that personal relationships between someone associated with your agency and a funder are golden and must be treated with respect.
- Guard against skirting a funder's established procedures for submitting a proposal.
- Know that in many circumstances, the relationship between a nonprofit agency and a funder begins with the submission of a grant proposal or letter of inquiry.

The Short Story

Writing Letters of Inquiry

I have made this letter longer than usual, only because I have not had time to make it shorter." These words of the seventeenth-century French philosopher and mathematician Blaise Pascal (often misattributed to Mark Twain), can be rephrased and applied to the grantseeking field: I didn't have time to write a letter of inquiry, so I wrote a proposal instead. If proposals are like novels, then letters are like short stories. Whereas novels can be long, meandering, and filled with subplots, short stories must be tightly compact, using an economy of words. Admittedly, it's challenging to keep your narrative brief. Every word counts. This chapter will demonstrate how to write a concise, persuasive, and successful letter of inquiry.

PURPOSE OF THE LETTER OF INQUIRY

Some grantmakers prefer to read a shortened version of your agency's story before receiving the full-length tale, and will invite you to submit a letter of inquiry (also called a letter of intent or LOI) prior to the submission of a full proposal. Think of an LOI as the first hoop you must jump through. The purpose of an LOI is to serve as a screening device for the funder. Grantmakers use LOIs to filter out requests that do not fit within their giving priorities or are otherwise not likely to be funded.

Using LOIs to screen applicants is a sound timesaving practice for both grant-makers and grantseekers. On the grantmaking side, a funder only needs to read a brief version of the agency's story in order to decide whether or not to invite the submission of a full proposal. On the grantseeking side, a nonprofit agency only needs to prepare a succinct letter to start the ball rolling. I know I joked that writing "short" can take more time than writing "long." And although there is some truth to this statement, the reality is that pulling together a full proposal (narrative and various attachments) is a time-consuming process, requiring even more time than preparing a well-crafted LOI.

An LOI is very brief, typically just one to three pages in length. If requesting an LOI, grantmakers often will specify the desired number of pages. If they don't, err on the side of brevity. Most often, an LOI is written on your agency's letterhead. A funder may ask for an LOI and only an LOI. It is also not unusual for a funder to ask for a few attachments to accompany the LOI, typically a program budget, your agency's annual budget, and board list. Gathering these attachments is never as time-consuming as it is when preparing attachments to accompany a full proposal.

How do you know whether or not to begin with an LOI? If the grantmaker says to, then I always do. Directions regarding how to initially approach a funder are most often found in the funder's guidelines on its Web site. For those funders that don't specify whether applicants should first submit an LOI, I recommend going straight to a full proposal. It is critical to always follow funders' instructions regarding what they want.

THE KEY WORD IS *FIT*

A successful LOI demonstrates that the agency is a good fit with the funder's current giving priorities. A persuasive LOI entices the funder to want to learn more. And the only way to obtain more information about the proposed project is to invite your agency to submit a full proposal.

To prepare a compelling LOI, you must present a fairly well-developed program idea. This is a topic I discuss in Chapter One. Although at this stage you don't need to have every detail fleshed out, the more specific you can be, the more substantial your LOI will be, and the more likely you are to be invited to proceed to the next step. If your LOI is vague, general rather than specific, conceptual rather than concrete, it won't be successful.

How do you demonstrate "fit"? To state the obvious: say so. It is entirely appropriate to tell the funder that you have read its guidelines and reviewed its list of recent grantees and that your agency is in alignment with the types of organizations currently being funded. Straight out. Just like that. But don't just say it. Show it. Describe what your agency is going to do and what it plans to accomplish so that the funder can see that there is a genuine fit. Examples 3.1 and 3.2 are a couple of excerpts that illustrate how to incorporate "fit" in an LOI. Note that the first also appropriately acknowledges the grantmaker's prior giving to the applicant agency.

HOW TO CRAFT A LETTER OF INQUIRY

Like short stories, LOIs have a beginning, a middle, and an end. As demonstrated in Examples 3.1 and 3.2, in the opening paragraph (or paragraphs) of an LOI, you should state why your agency is a good fit with the potential funder and acknowledge prior funding (if applicable). The lead paragraph is often also a good place to tell the funder how much money your agency now seeks and for what purpose.

Further, if other grantmakers have already committed support to the program, be sure to weave that information into your LOI story. Frequently I will list a few of the funders who are most widely known and will thus lend greater credibility to a project. I refer to them as "marquee" funders whose names you want to display in metaphoric bright lights in your proposal, typically in the paragraph discussing the amount of the ask and total cost of the project. As you are probably well aware, the first grant dollars are the most difficult ones for any nonprofit agency to raise. Once an agency secures initial funding, additional funders are more apt to come aboard. That's because when a program already has committed funding, new prospective grantmakers know that their funding colleagues have determined that the program is worthy of support.

State the specific dollar amount your agency plans to request from the grantmaker if your agency is invited to submit a full proposal. Make certain that this amount is within the funder's customary range (which is another indication that the request is a good fit). State the program's overall budget so that the funder can see what percentage (100 percent or some lesser amount) it is being asked to provide. This also makes it clear to the grantmaker whether the requesting agency is asking for a lead or cornerstone gift or for the funder to participate to a lesser degree.

Example 3.1
Letter of Inquiry Excerpt Demonstrating "Fit" for an Adolescent Behavioral Health Program

Dear Trustee:

In the mid-1990s, the Generous Fund was a supporter of the Patterson Adolescent Behavioral Health Program ("Patterson Program") at Rincon Valley Medical Center. We deeply appreciate this past generosity and hope we can renew the Fund's interest in our work with youth (ages 12 to 21) who suffer from severe mental illness. We believe that the Patterson Program is a good fit with the Generous Fund, given the Fund's philanthropic support for human and social services, specifically those programs that help children and teens. Therefore, we write this LOI to tell you about our need to purchase various library, art, and recreational items so that we may better serve our young patients. The total cost of these items is $40,000, and we would request a $10,000 grant from the Generous Fund if encouraged to submit a full proposal.

Example 3.2
Letter of Inquiry Excerpt Demonstrating "Fit" for a Faith-Based Volunteer Program

Dear Trustee:

Given the E. & S. Fisher Foundation's support of Catholic agencies and those that address the needs of the poor, I am writing to tell you about the Jesuit Volunteer Corps: Southwest. If invited to submit a full proposal, we will request a grant of $15,000. These funds will be used to provide support services to 25 young adult volunteers who are working with, and living among, the poor and marginalized in the San Francisco Bay Area. Our volunteers are "on fire" with a desire to make a difference. I hope that the E. & S. Fisher Foundation will provide one of the sparks to make this happen!

What should your approach be if no grant funds have yet been raised? My suggestion is that you acknowledge this reality. In these circumstances, I have used language similar to the following: "We invite your foundation to provide crucial leadership support for our agency's new initiative."

In the next paragraph or two of an LOI, establish your agency's credibility, then briefly describe what the problem is and how your agency plans to respond. You may want to include one or two key statistics. Choose ones that either frame the scope of the problem or give it a context within your community. Next, describe the likely results your agency hopes to achieve. This section of an LOI serves to answer the question, What difference will your agency make in the lives of the people it serves?

At the end of the LOI, thank the funder for considering your agency's request. It is a good idea to provide the name of a contact person at your agency in case the funder has any questions or needs additional information. LOIs should be signed by the agency's executive director, the chair of the board of directors, or both. (In other words, the agency's senior administrator should sign the LOI, and this may be a head of school, dean, or artistic director, as appropriate.) Because your executive director or other senior administrator may not be readily available to respond to inquiries from the funder, consider designating your agency's development director or grantwriter as the agency's primary contact person for follow-up questions.

The preceding paragraphs have provided a structure for crafting a letter of intent. Add vivid, compelling language, and you'll have an effective LOI. Choose your words carefully. Be precise. Be specific, rather than general. And leave a little mystery. You want to provide enough information that the funder will conclude that your request is in alignment with its funding interests, but you don't want to give so much information that you'll have nothing new to say if invited to submit a full proposal. Your goal is to leave the funder wanting to know more, which are the details that you'll be able to include in a proposal.

Examples 3.3 and 3.4 are two well-crafted LOIs that illustrate the points covered in this chapter. The first is from a retirement center discussing its need for a shuttle bus to transport senior residents on errands, appointments, and recreational trips. The second is from an environmental organization concerning species preservation.

Example 3.3
Letter of Inquiry from a Retirement Center for Equipment Purchase

Nancy Krickl
Program Officer
Famously Foods Company Foundation

Dear Ms. Krickl:

One of the life-altering moments for an elderly person is the day that individual stops driving an automobile. Immediately, there is a sense of lost freedom and independence. At The Grove, a not-for-profit retirement community that serves a predominantly low- and middle-income population, we want to provide our senior residents with a transportation alternative that is safe, affordable, convenient, and flexible. Our goal is to purchase a 16-passenger, wheelchair-accessible shuttle bus to serve our 330 residents. The cost of a new shuttle bus is nearly $58,000. To date, we have received $32,000 from foundations and individuals. We now seek the remaining $16,000 to make this goal a reality. Famously Foods Company is a leader in the local business community and is known for supporting nonprofit retirement communities, which is why we write this letter of inquiry.

Currently, residents at The Grove have the following transportation options. Some still own and operate their own automobiles, though the majority do not. Some rely on friends and family. Some use public transportation, and a few use taxis. Yet each of these alternatives has its limitations. Driving is not an option for most of our residents. Friends and family are not always available. Public transportation is limited. Taxis are expensive. A center-owned shuttle bus will help meet a very critical transportation need for our seniors, enabling them to shop, do their banking, visit the library, get to doctor's appointments, attend church services, and go on recreational excursions. We anticipate grouping daily trips geographically to be energy and time efficient.

Longer excursions may take residents to museums and on other cultural outings.

In a recent survey of The Grove community, 166 residents indicated that they would use a center-owned shuttle bus as their primary transportation option if one were available. Of these 166 residents, 92 are nondrivers, and 74 still own and operate their own cars.

The Grove was founded in 1965 and is located on a 14-acre campus that offers four levels of care, from independent living to health care. Our residents range in age from 66 to nearly 105, with the average age being 85. Sixty percent of our residents are low and middle income, and our community is among the most affordable in the region. Consistent with our mission to provide affordable senior housing, private financial support and government subsidies are presently given to 65 residents who live on small pensions, social security, and modest savings.

The environment at The Grove is active and celebrates life. A new shuttle bus will enable our residents to more fully access nearby stores and services, as well as area-wide cultural outings. We hope the Famously Foods Company Foundation will be interested in learning more about our community and our need for a new transportation alternative for our residents, and will invite us to submit a full proposal. If you have any questions or need additional information, please call our Director of Development and Communications, Margaret Hansen, or me. Thank you very much for your consideration of our request.

Sincerely,

Ronald Yee
Executive Director

Example 3.4
Letter of Inquiry from an Environmental Agency for Program Support

Ms. Jean Therrien
President
The Therrien Family Foundation
123 Main Street
Central City, OH 45678

Dear Ms. Therrien:

Because The Therrien Family Foundation is well known for supporting causes that promote species preservation and animal welfare, I am writing this letter of inquiry to introduce you to the work being done by Save the Three-Toed Lizard, a 501(c)(3) organization based in Central City. Save the Three-Toed Lizard is dedicated to preserving this majestic amphibian and to saving its ever-decreasing habitat here in Ohio.

We would like to submit a grant proposal for $25,000 to support our Three-Toed Lizard Awareness and Preservation Campaign for the Greater Central City Area. The budget for this campaign is $175,000, and to date we have raised nearly $80,000, including commitments from the Miller Ecology Fund, Big Bank in Town, and Major Corporation.

Save the Three-Toed Lizard was established in 1981 by dedicated biologists, naturalists, and other volunteers who were alarmed by the rapid loss of lizard habitat due to urban growth and development. For twenty years, our organization has worked diligently to save this precious species and its dwindling habitat through educational programs, lobbying activities, and community outreach. As you may know, the Greater Central City Area is one of the prime breeding grounds for the lizard. However, suburban encroachment threatens to drastically reduce the few acres of breeding ground that remain.

In response to this current threat, Save the Three-Toed Lizard intends to launch an area-wide campaign to raise public awareness of the importance of the species and its fragile habitat. We plan a multipronged approach, which includes making appearances before local zoning boards and other land use decision makers and preparing public awareness materials (such as public service announcements and fliers). We hope that the Therrien Family Foundation agrees that this is a problem deserving immediate attention, and we hope to be invited to submit a full proposal to tell you more about the proposed work of Save the Three-Toed Lizard.

I appreciate your consideration of this letter and look forward to hearing from the foundation soon. If you have any questions, please contact either our Development Director, Cathy Doligalski, or me at 123-456-7890.

Sincerely,

Justine Moorehouse
Executive Director

SUMMARY

Writing a letter of inquiry can be challenging due to the constraints on length. You must pack a lot of information into just a couple of pages at most. In this chapter, I've provided a structure for organizing an LOI and discussed what information is really important to funders, and why, in reviewing LOIs. The following are key points to remember:

- Submit an LOI when the funder requests one; otherwise you can proceed with a full proposal.
- Think of an LOI as a timesaving device for both you and the funder, and as one step in the grantseeking process.
- Demonstrate "fit" between a funder's priorities and the program for which you are seeking funding.
- Provide enough information in your LOI to entice the funder to want to learn more about your agency and proposed project.

The Proposal Narrative

Introducing the Characters and the Place

I f a letter of inquiry is akin to a short story, then a proposal narrative is analogous to a novel. When I first started working in the nonprofit field nearly two decades ago, proposal narratives often were of epic length, some as long as fifteen, twenty, even twenty-five pages. Today, in response to changing funder requirements and the use of online submissions, we write slimmer stories that typically run between five to ten pages in length, occasionally even shorter. There's a lot of information that must be packed in these relatively few pages. For a proposal to rise out of the "slush pile" of other sub-missions, it must engage the reader by being well written and telling a compelling story. From the opening sentence, the narrative must grab the reader's attention and hold it through till the end. It's all about telling a good story.

OPEN WITH A "HOOK"

Outstanding storytellers engage the audience with that first word or sentence. It's the "hook" that pulls the reader into the story. The same is true in proposal writing. A talented proposal writer uses strong, not gimmicky, prose. Avoid openings that are too cute, too clever, or too cliché. For example, it is *never* a good idea to begin a proposal with the following: "No nonprofit agency is an island; no nonprofit agency stands alone. This is why we write to the XYZ Foundation." Ugh.

I also advise you to refrain from relying on what I call "comfort language" to begin your proposal. I am referring to those safe, polite, and inoffensive phrases and sentences we tend to fall back on when we're not sure what to say—sentences like these: "We are pleased to respectfully submit this proposal to the Doyle Family Fund." Yawn. I'm guilty of writing sentences like this myself, and although a plain-as-vanilla opening is serviceable, you run the risk of putting the reader to sleep and not engaging him or her in your story.

I recommend an alternative. I suggest that you be bolder and consider a more creative approach. When looking for an effective hook, I think about using one of three possible options: the attention-grabbing fact, the key question, or the quote from an expert. Here's how each option might be used as the opening in a proposal requesting funds to support a breast cancer awareness campaign.

- One in eight women will be diagnosed with breast cancer in Marin County, which has one of the highest breast cancer rates in the country.
- Did you know that Marin County has one of the highest breast cancer rates in the country?
- "Marin County's alarmingly high breast cancer rate is our number one public health issue," says Isaac Roth, MD, oncologist and author of a groundbreaking study recently published in the *New England Journal of Medicine*.

Each of these alternative openings fulfills two important objectives: each engages the reader, and each delivers key information. This is crucial when you have limited space in which to tell your story, either due to length restrictions or the constraints of an online application.

Keep in mind that whenever you present a fact, a number, or a statistic in a proposal, you should consider whether or not you also need to cite the source of the information. In the preceding example, you may want to cite the study or report that determined that one out of eight women will be diagnosed with breast cancer in Marin County. When including quotes, be mindful of the statement's relevancy to the topic and the speaker's credibility. Include a quote only when it is expressly to the point and supports your case. And the more credible the individual, the more credible the statement. As illustrated in the example, an oncologist-researcher-author is qualified to comment on the seriousness of breast cancer in a given community.

Time to Write!

Now it's time for you to try your hand at writing a new lead sentence for one of your proposals. See if you can use *each* variation—a key fact, a question, and a quote—in writing a "hook" for your next proposal. Consider which option best suits your particular needs.

Example 4.1
Intro for a Girls Sports Program

"Everything good in me died in junior high" (from *Reviving Ophelia: Saving the Selves of Adolescent Girls,* by Mary Pipher).

Despite advances in gender equality in the latter half of the twentieth century, American adolescent girls of all socioeconomic backgrounds continue to experience a steep decline in self-esteem in middle school and junior high. Studies link this decline to the epidemic levels of depression and eating disorders that we are witnessing today among adolescent and teen girls. These problems are in addition to alarming levels of substance abuse, violent crime, sexual risk-taking, lower academic achievement, and other social and personal problems.

According to Dr. Mary Pipher, clinical psychologist and author of the hugely popular recent book *Reviving Ophelia: Saving the Selves of Adolescent Girls,* ours is a beauty-obsessed, media-driven, "girl-poisoning" culture that ultimately destroys girls' self-esteem. More often than not, girls blame themselves or their families for their "failures" instead of looking at the world around them.

Remarkably, there is one activity that can greatly offset the emotional and psychological debilitation of adolescent girls—and that is sports. SportsBridge is one of a handful of organizations around the United States that is devoted to utilizing sports as a vehicle to build the self-esteem of adolescent girls.

Note: These are the opening paragraphs of a proposal for SportsBridge, a program that paired eighth-grade girls from urban middle schools with athletes and sports enthusiasts for a year of one-on-one mentoring and group activities, including outings to college and professional sporting events. This excerpt was contributed by Nancy E. Quinn, principal in Nancy E. Quinn Associates, a consulting firm specializing in arts management and fundraising.

Example 4.2
Intro for a Blood Bank

During the first two weeks of the year, the San Francisco Bay Area faced a critical health care emergency. Blood Centers of the Pacific's (BCP's) inventory of blood had fallen alarmingly low. Blood donations typically drop during the holidays. This decrease, coupled with a nationwide blood shortage that prevented importing blood into the region, created a perilous situation. On January 5, BCP asked local hospitals to cancel and postpone surgeries due to the acute shortage of blood, specifically Type-O blood.

With help from the local media, BCP sent out an emergency appeal for blood donations. Within a 14-day period, BCP collected 5,412 units of blood—an increase of almost 50% from the average collection of 3,700 units. By January 10, BCP was able to advise hospitals that they could resume normal surgery schedules.

What those two weeks illustrate is the challenge BCP faces in maintaining an adequate supply of blood. BCP seeks to reverse the trend of blood donations not keeping pace with the demand. Through broader community outreach and education efforts, we hope to recruit significantly more Bay Area residents to give blood in the coming years.

A strong opening sentence entices the reader to read the next sentence, the next paragraph, and so on. Subsequent paragraphs build on the foundation laid by those initial sentences. To show you what I mean, I've included three examples of powerful introductions (see Examples 4.1, 4.2, and 4.3).

PRESENT FUNDAMENTAL INFORMATION

Your proposal must not only grab the reader's attention with the first few sentences and paragraphs but should also provide the potential funder with some essential information. The majority of reviewers expect to see the following three questions addressed early in a proposal:

• What are the history and mission of the applicant agency?

• Who are the agency's clients?

• Where do the clients reside, and where does the agency do its work?

> ## Example 4.3
> ## Intro for a Wildlife Preservation Group
>
> ---
>
> It was a classic "sting" operation. Two undercover law enforcement officers arrange to meet a buyer. At the meeting, they show the buyer the booty they have harvested in the remote reaches of Northern California. Once the buyer pays for the contraband and places another order for more of the same, the two officers reveal their identities, make the arrest, and seize key records that lead them to an extensive ring of deals.
>
> This is an all-too-familiar scenario, but this "bust" is different. The harvest being offered for sale isn't drugs, but animal parts. Bear paws and gallbladders. Mountain lion heads. And the two officers are game wardens posing not as marijuana growers but as commercial poachers. And the buyer is dealing in animal parts, which are then processed and sold as aphrodisiacs, medicinal potions, trophies, and gourmet cuisine.
>
> Such poaching activity is a growing problem in wilderness areas across the country. It threatens to destroy a valuable natural resource—our protected wildlife.
>
> The Mountain Lion Foundation, a nonprofit organization dedicated to the protection of mountain lions and other wildlife and their habitats, plans to launch an antipoaching campaign to stop the slaughter of wildlife for illegal profit in California. With foundation and other private support, we plan to attack poaching at every turn, using skills and grassroots support built by the Mountain Lion Foundation over the years.
>
> *Note:* This highly creative opening was written by fundraising consultant Susan Fox, my coauthor for *Grant Proposal Makeover: Transform Your Request from No to Yes.*

In fact, many grantmakers will specifically ask that the proposal answer these questions. Once again, it is beneficial if you can respond to these questions using an economy of words. Let's look at how to address these three basic questions in more detail.

Introduce the Hero

One of the delights of proposal writing is whom and what you write about. The nonprofit sector is a noble one. People who have chosen to work in the field are passionate, dedicated, intelligent, and creative. The people being served by non-profit agencies are typically a rich cast of characters, and they are the primary focus of your agency's proposals. These are your story's main characters. Yet the first "character" introduced in the proposal narrative is generally not the clients your agency serves. In fact, this character is not a person at all. But it is the hero of the story.

Who, or rather what, is the hero in your proposal narrative? It's your non-profit agency! Nonprofit agencies do heroic work, and they are the heroes in every proposal we write. Throughout the world today, nonprofits are working diligently to feed the hungry, shelter the homeless, heal the sick, teach children, conserve the environment, save endangered species, and present music per-formances and art exhibitions, among other important activities. There is tre-mendous drama and excitement in stories from the nonprofit community. As grantwriters, we have an opportunity to tell others these amazing stories.

The reason we introduce the hero (the nonprofit agency) early in our pro-posal stories is to establish the agency's credibility with the funder. The objective is to demonstrate to the grantmaker that the agency has the ability to success-fully do the work for which it is seeking funding. One of the best ways to do this is by describing the agency's most relevant and most outstanding prior achieve-ments and accomplishments. The underlying message is that if the agency has accomplished great things in the past, it is likely to continue to accomplish great things in the future. The agency has credibility.

Consider a contemporary hero known to just about everyone on the planet: Harry Potter. In the early chapters of the popular Harry Potter books, the author, J. K. Rowling, places young Potter in situations where he demonstrates that he has courage, mental and physical strength, and fierce determination. Given Potter's innate abilities, readers are not surprised to see the boy (and later, teen) heroically, and ultimately successfully, battling dark forces at the end of each book. We've been given enough information earlier in the book to believe that Harry Potter is a credible hero and that he's up to the challenge of whatever per-ils he faces. If the author had not provided us with this information and insight into Potter's character and abilities, we'd be surprised, perhaps even disbelieving, of Potter's heroism.

How then do you apply the "Harry Potter principle" to a grant proposal? By showing early on in the proposal that your nonprofit agency has heroic qualities.

This is done in what is often called the "history and mission" or "introduction" section of the grant proposal. (In fact, expect to see the following question presented in one form or another in many grant applications and guidelines: What is your agency's history and mission?) In the history-mission-introductory section you answer this question. (For simplicity's sake, I'll refer to this portion of the proposal as the introduction.)

This is the part of the proposal where you get to "toot your agency's horn." State when the agency was founded and by whom, what its mission is, what its major accomplishments and achievements have been, how many clients it has served, and whether it has received recognition for its good work through awards or acclamation. Resist the urge to provide a laundry list of achievements and accolades. Rather, curb this tendency by providing only the most relevant, current, and important information. Your task is to give the reader enough information to conclude that the agency is well qualified for the next task, the one for which you are seeking funding. No more is necessary.

How Long Should the Introduction Be?

The introduction section is not a lengthy one. Keep the introduction in proportion to the proposal's overall length. I estimate that a typical introduction will comprise between 5 and 10 percent of the total proposal length. In a five-page narrative, this means a paragraph or two, and certainly no more than a half page.

What may be counterintuitive is the fact that the older your agency is, the shorter the introductory section needs to be; more recently established agencies (and grassroots agencies) require longer introductions. The reason is this: agencies that have been around for a while are more apt to be known in the community. For these agencies, their reputations precede their proposals. The most venerable agencies wear a halo of credibility, so less needs to be said to convince a funder that they will be prudent stewards of future grant funding.

In rare cases, however, being too well known can have a downside—for example, if the community holds negative misperceptions about a nonprofit agency. You will need to address and correct these misperceptions in the proposal narrative, and certainly this will lengthen the introductory section.

Similarly, new agencies, grassroots agencies, and agencies with low visibility are likely to need lengthier introductions in order to establish credibility.

Establishing Credibility for a Start-Up Agency

What do you do if your nonprofit agency is a brand-new start-up? In this situation, you establish your agency's credibility by presenting the qualifications of the nonprofit's founders. The educational backgrounds, professional expertise, and work experience of these individuals substitute for a well-established agency's accomplishments over many years. The more credible an agency's founders are, the more likely it is that the new agency will be able to secure initial grant funding.

Generally speaking, grantmakers are skeptical when they receive a grant request from an organization that has only one, two, or a handful of active supporters. The funder suspects it is being asked to support the pet project of an individual or a small group of individuals. Funders prefer to support nonprofit agencies that enjoy broad community support. Wider support indicates that the community need is great and demonstrates that several people are committed to addressing this need. If you're thinking about forming a nonprofit organization, make certain that others share your vision before you begin to seek grant funding.

Example 4.4
Introducing the Well-Established Hero: A Music School

Since its founding in 1920 by two dedicated piano instructors, the Zosseder Conservatory of Music has contributed to the rich musical life of our city, the state, and the world beyond. Today the conservatory is an internationally respected, fully accredited four-year college of music. We have an outstanding faculty and an exceptionally talented student body of 1,500 students who represent 50 states and 23 countries. Our graduates include numerous renowned performing artists and conductors, including Johann Sebastian Bach, Ludwig van Beethoven, and Wolfgang Amadeus Mozart. The conservatory currently offers undergraduate degrees in fifteen major disciplines—from classical guitar to jazz performance. *U.S. News & World Report* recently ranked the Zosseder Conservatory of Music as the number one undergraduate music school in the country, topping the list of 50 other contenders.

Introducing the Hero: Examples

Examples 4.4 and 4.5 show how to introduce your proposal's hero—the nonprofit agency—in the proposal narrative. The first example is for a well-established, highly visible institution, and the second is for a brand-new grassroots organization.

The single paragraph in Example 4.4 is all that is necessary to establish the Zosseder Conservatory of Music's credibility. The school has been around for a

---

Example 4.5
Introducing a New Hero: A Youth Agency

Meditation for Minors is a new 501(c)(3) not-for-profit agency whose mission is to teach meditation and other relaxation techniques to young people who are either in juvenile hall or on probation. By voluntarily participating in our program, teens will learn peaceful alternative ways of coping with anger and stress. Meditation for Minors was founded by Dr. Clara Voyant, a highly regarded yoga instructor. Dr. Voyant is the founder and owner of Clara's Yoga School, where for the past 15 years she has taught thousands of adults and teens. She is also the author of *Yoga for Youngsters*.

Four years ago, Ted Johnson, sheriff of Juniper County, took one of Dr. Voyant's classes. After a few weeks of instruction, Sheriff Johnson commented to Dr. Voyant that many of the troubled youth he encountered could benefit from a program like hers. Dr. Voyant saw an exciting opportunity. Working with Sheriff Johnson, senior administrators at the county juvenile hall, and other police officers, Dr. Voyant created a pilot program to reach youth who were serving time in juvenile hall. The pilot program was successful, reaching some 50 young people. Last year Dr. Voyant received the Mayor's Award for Volunteerism, and the city's probation department asked Dr. Voyant to create a similar program for youth on probation.

To respond to the growing need, Dr. Voyant and five other community leaders, including Sheriff Johnson, formed the initial board of directors and established Meditation for Minors.

---

long time and is accredited. It has illustrious graduates, a strong faculty, and a geographically diverse student body. And it achieved the top spot in a popular ranking of U.S. music colleges. Given these credentials, it can be presumed that this institution is qualified to teach the next generation of music students.

In contrast, note how much more is needed to provide the qualifications and accomplishments of a grassroots agency, Meditation for Minors, in Example 4.5.

As you can see in Example 4.5, more detail is necessary when an organization is brand new. And because the agency itself is too new to have a track record, the proposal writer substitutes the founder's credentials as an established yoga teacher and author, as well as the credibility offered through the participation of Sheriff Johnson, to establish credibility.

Advice About Mission Statements

It is not unusual for a grantmaker to request that an agency provide information about its mission in the proposal. The question then arises as to whether or not to include the agency's actual mission statement. My advice is this: if your agency has a succinct and compelling mission statement, you probably can include it verbatim. For many nonprofits, the reality is that their mission statements are neither succinct nor compelling. Too often, the mission statements I see are long, vague, and uninspiring. These mission statements are not going to help advance an agency's case for support. When faced with this reality, I rephrase the deficient mission statement into language that is far more passionate and compelling while remaining faithful to the agency's mission.

Time to Write!

Whether you work for a large, long-established institution or a new, grassroots agency, the "history and mission" or introductory section in a proposal demonstrates that your agency is credible and capable. Write at least three facts or factual statements about your agency's history or its major achievements and accomplishments. If motivated, write an entire introduction. You'll get extra credit if you do!

INTRODUCE THE OTHER MAIN CHARACTERS

The best stories feature characters we want to read about. Stories, whether real or fictional, are most memorable when they present compelling, believable characters. Think of Oliver Twist, Scarlett O'Hara, and Sherlock Holmes. The authors who created these iconic characters (Dickens, Mitchell, and Doyle, respectively) made them fascinating by giving them vivid personalities and distinctive traits. These are such engrossing characters that we'd follow them through chapters of travails and triumphs. Similarly, grantseekers must also present characters who are engaging to the reader. But unlike fiction writers, those of us who write grant proposals do not need to create characters from our imaginations. Rather, the main characters in a grant proposal are the real-life clients served by the nonprofit agency. And these individuals are every bit as fascinating, complex, and engaging as Tom Sawyer, Huckleberry Finn, and Becky Thatcher.

Writing About the Other Main Characters

In addition to introducing the nonprofit agency early in the proposal, grantseekers should also give the reader a little information about the story's other lead characters, namely, the agency's clients. Consider this a bit of foreshadowing, because these main characters will be revisited as the proposal's plot progresses, specifically in the needs or problem statement section of a proposal.

At the beginning of your proposal narrative, it is important for the reader to know what segment of the population is principally served by the agency. Does your agency provide services for the frail elderly? Youth at risk? Gays and lesbians? Elementary school children? Recent immigrants? People with certain health care needs? In other words, how does your agency define its primary constituency? Would this population remain the same if the agency received the requested grant funding, or would the agency expand its services to an additional segment of the population?

It is a very rare nonprofit agency that can legitimately claim to serve everyone. The world and its population are too big, and there are too many issues to address. Defining the client population narrows the scope. It shows the funder that the agency has identified which specific characters, out of the larger global cast, it serves. Having a defined client population also further demonstrates agency credibility because only a naive nonprofit agency or a very unusual one can honestly boast that it offers programs to meet the needs of every single person in every single community.

Writing About Main Characters Other Than People

So far, I've talked only about clients (characters) who are people. Yet primary "clients" are not always limited to the human race. Clients can also be injured marine mammals, old-growth redwood trees, or coral reefs. As grantwriters, we nevertheless must relate the significance of serving animals or plants back to people. Why is it important for an agency to serve the needs of marine mammals, majestic redwoods, or colorful coral reefs? When you work with a non-profit agency that deals with rehabilitating wild animals or preserving natural habitats, your grant proposal must discuss the impact these creatures or the environment has on the human population. For example, what will be lost if the white rhino becomes extinct? Why should people care if the wetlands cease to exist? If your proposal doesn't address questions like these, it is too easy for the reader simply to shrug and say, "So what?"—and then go on to the next proposal. Example 4.6 illustrates how an environmental agency effectively deals with this issue.

Example 4.6
When Clients Aren't People: Excerpt from an
Environmental Agency Proposal

For generations, Northern Californians and others from across the country and around the world have vacationed, recreated, and relaxed at Lake Tahoe. However, burgeoning development and certain land management practices are damaging the health of the Lake Tahoe Basin's pristine environment. The mission of the League to Save Lake Tahoe is to find solutions to these serious issues.

Our goal is to "Keep Tahoe Blue" for future generations of visitors. Yet time is running out. Studies indicate that lake clarity is declining at an alarming rate, currently losing an average of a foot of clarity each year. Because the reasons for the loss of lake clarity are complex, the League is involved in numerous activities, which include administrative advocacy, public investment, and grassroots education.

ESTABLISH A SENSE OF TIME AND PLACE

Just as good storytellers do, grantwriters must become adept at establishing a sense of time and place.

Creating a Sense of Time

Unlike fiction writers, who can spin tales about the past, present, or far into the distant future, proposal writers always write about the relatively near future. This is a maxim in grantseeking. Why? Because grantmakers will not fund an agency's prior work or activities. Foundations and corporations award grants to support *future* programs. Grantseeking is prospective. Therefore, you write proposals to secure funding for programs and activities that will be undertaken six months, a year, or, at the outside, perhaps two or three years in the future.

For this reason, it is critical for nonprofit agencies to plan ahead. Those nonprofit agencies following "best practices" within the field will periodically undertake a strategic planning process and formulate a strategic plan. Having a written strategic plan makes grantseeking that much easier. Without a comprehensive strategic plan, an agency is more likely to launch one ill-conceived program after another, reacting to potential funding opportunities rather than developing well-conceived programs and then proactively seeking the grant funding to support them.

Foundation and corporate grantmakers generally award grants for a one-year period. Some grantmakers offer multiyear funding—for a two- or three-year period, but never longer. This means that the time period discussed in our narrative proposals is a relatively short one and corresponds to the likely grant period. If you're seeking one-year grant funding, then you describe the work your agency will be doing in that corresponding one-year period. For simplicity and accounting ease, I recommend using your agency's fiscal year. In other words, when requesting grant funds, tell the funder what your agency will be doing and how the funds will be used to do it during a specific fiscal year. If it is early in your fiscal year (within the first six months), you are likely to be seeking funding that can be applied to the present fiscal year. However, if you are midway or more through a fiscal year, you are likely to be requesting funds for the next one.

When doing any sort of financial and cash flow planning, remember that you need to allow time for funders to read and evaluate submitted proposals. A cash grant does not arrive a day or a week or even a month after you submit your request. The proposal review process can take anywhere from two months (very fast track) to twelve months or more (in rare cases, as long as eighteen months). In my experience, the average review time is four to six months.

Creating a Sense of Place

Location, location, location. Those are the three most important words in real estate. Location is also an important concept to convey in a grant proposal. If the location is aptly described, the reader visualizes where the agency is doing its work and clients are being served. In a well-written proposal, you can figuratively bring a potential funder to the community in which your agency operates its programs—whether it is an inner-city neighborhood or a sparsely populated rural setting.

For fiction writers, the setting can be a gritty urban neighborhood or a desolate mountain range. It can be a foreign land or a setting as familiar as our own backyard. Similarly, the locations of our proposal stories vary greatly. This leads to another maxim in grantseeking: it is essential for your proposal to state where the nonprofit agency does its work. Why? Because as we discussed in Chapter Two, the vast majority of grantmakers set geographic boundaries for their grantmaking and will fund only those agencies that work and serve clients in a defined region. A funder may limit its grantmaking to a specific neighborhood, city, a county, a few counties, a region within a state (such as Northern California), a state, a region within the United States (such as the Pacific Northwest), a country, or a hemisphere. There are extremely rare cases where funders make grants to nonprofit agencies operating in any corner of the world. Corporate grantmakers tend to be especially firm about funding in specifically defined geographic areas, usually in communities where they are headquartered, operate manufacturing facilities, or have significant business operations.

Because grantmakers often use geography as a criterion when making funding decisions, it is wise to establish a sense of place early in your proposal narrative. This is another key way you can demonstrate to the funder that your agency fits within the funder's giving standards.

Examples 4.7 and 4.8 do an especially fine job of describing location.

Example 4.7
Describing the Location of a Rural Retreat Center

We write to request grant funding for a special capital project—to help renovate and restore "Our Lady of the Oaks," a family-friendly, affordable Catholic retreat center nestled in the Sierra foothills. The Province acquired the 360-acre Oaks Retreat in the mid-1950s and renamed the site Our Lady of the Oaks. For nearly 50 years, the Province has operated the facility as a retreat and conference center, serving predominantly Catholic and Catholic-affiliated groups. Our Lady of the Oaks, which is also known as Applegate Villa, is located an hour's drive east of Sacramento, just off I-80. To maintain affordability, Our Lady of the Oaks is decidedly rustic, yet comfortable. Most bedrooms sleep two, and all have shared bathrooms. There are more than a dozen buildings on the site, several dating back to the early 1900s when the original Oaks Retreat was a popular getaway lodge. Current buildings include the rickety main "Old Lodge," the Main Lodge, a half dozen rustic cabins, a serene chapel, a conference room, a kitchen/dining hall, and administrative offices. The site also features an outdoor swimming pool and volleyball nets. Meals are served family-style in the dining room.

But the real attraction of Our Lady of the Oaks is its natural beauty. The center is located among pines and oaks at about 2,000-foot elevation in the Sierra foothills. A short walk from the main lodging facilities is a tranquil pond. Our Lady of the Oaks provides an ideal location for personal reflection, spiritual renewal, and contemplation. It is a place where people can escape from the pressing demands of daily life and rejuvenate. The center enables groups to come together, to refocus, to reflect, and to plan. Departing groups emerge reenergized and better prepared for work and volunteerism.

Both of the excerpts in Examples 4.7 and 4.8 do a fine job of transporting the reader to a physical place. In the first example, it is a rustic retreat center nestled in the Sierra foothills. In the second, it is the inner city. Where do your proposals take the funder?

For our city's homeless population, life on the streets is rough and down-right dangerous. Drug dealing, prostitution, and other criminal activity flourish around those individuals taking shelter in doorways and under freeway ramps. There are no available bathrooms, no toilets, showers, or sinks. To get a daily hot meal, one must line up early in front of the soup kitchen on 6th Avenue. With winter approaching, for many homeless individuals there's a greater urgency to find one of the coveted spaces in overnight shelters. For others, the arrival of colder days and nights just means putting on more layers of clothes. From our bustling building on Chicago's South Side, Helping Hands serves more than 1,000 nutritious hot meals daily and shelters up to 75 men and 25 women each night.

Time to Write!

Do your proposals adequately describe the geographic location and physical surroundings where your agency does its work? Here's a writing exercise for you to once again flex your writing muscle. I ask you to write three to five short phrases that paint a vivid picture of your agency's location.

SUMMARY

Some grant proposals seem to almost jump out of the pile of submissions and grab the reader from the very first word. Here's a review of the main points covered in this chapter; they can help your agency's proposals have the same captivating effect:

- Use a strong hook to grab and pull the reader into the story.
- Consider leading with an important fact, a key question, or a notable quote.
- Establish the credibility of your hero agency by describing prior accomplishments and achievements in the proposal's introduction section (also known as the "history and mission" section).

- Remember that not every mission statement is ready for "prime time" publication in a proposal.
- Specifically define the population being served by your agency. Your clients are the main characters in your proposal story. Describe what they have in common.
- Tell the funder where your agency does its work. Paint a vivid word picture of this location.
- Introduce the hero agency, the narrative's main characters (agency clients), and the physical setting early in your proposal story.

The Need or Problem

Building Tension and Conflict into Your Story

The plot thickens as we move further along in the grant proposal. Thus far, you've introduced the story's hero (your agency) and other main characters (agency clients). You've established the geographic setting. You may have foreshadowed that a problem exists. Now it's time to inject some real action into the narrative. This means unleashing the story's antagonist!

UNDERSTANDING THE STORY ARC

If one were to diagram a traditional story, the drawing would look a lot like a bell curve, a line gradually rising up, peaking, then falling back down. That would be a visual image of a story arc, which represents the unfolding of events (see Figure 5.1).

First, the storyteller invites the reader into the universe he or she has created. Characters are introduced. Time and setting are established. Then the story begins traveling up the arc with the introduction of conflict between the protagonist (the hero) and other lead characters on one side and the antagonist on the other. The drama unfolds. Tension begins to build. In the most compelling stories, the author brings readers to the edge of their seats.

Tension continues to mount until the tale reaches its climax. At this pivotal point, something significant, and usually dramatic, happens to one or more of

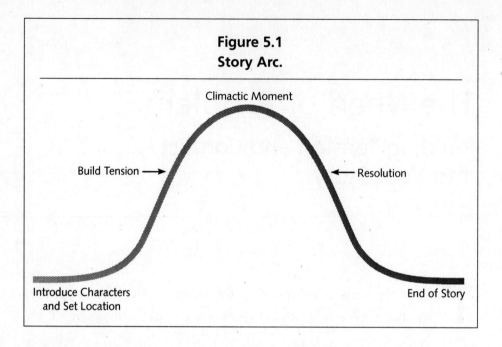

Figure 5.1
Story Arc.

Climactic Moment

Build Tension →   ← Resolution

Introduce Characters   End of Story
and Set Location

the main characters. Then the tension breaks. This is a cathartic moment, often for both the characters and the reader. What has occurred is so significant that the lives of one or more of the main characters will have changed forever. After this moment, the storyteller leads the reader back down the arc, providing a complete, satisfying resolution of the conflict and a wrap-up of the story.

In truly exceptional stories, something also happens to us as readers. Our view of the world changes. Outstanding grant proposals can have the same effect. They motivate a prospective funder to award a grant. And that's what it's all about.

In this chapter, I'll begin to describe the story arc in a grant proposal, showing how to build tension into your agency's proposal narratives. (In Chapter Six, I will deal with the story's actual climactic moment and demonstrate how to write a satisfying resolution.)

WHO IS THE ANTAGONIST?

Who is the antagonist in our proposal stories? Hint: it isn't a person. The antagonist is something larger than any single person. (Often something more diabolic than Sherlock Holmes's nemesis, Dr. Moriarty, and more terrifying than Harry

Potter's Lord Voldemort.) The antagonist in our proposal stories is the need or problem being addressed by our agency. The problem or need is frequently unwieldy and complex. And although we may have foreshadowed the problem at the beginning of our narrative (recall the important fact, key question, and notable quote from Chapter Four?), in this dedicated section in your proposal it is time to elaborate more fully.

If all were going well in our communities and if this were a perfect world, then there would be no reason for grantmakers and grantseekers to exist. Like dinosaurs, they would be rendered extinct. But everything is not okay in our communities. And this is not a perfect world. There are problems. Our communities have great, some would say overwhelming, needs. There are people who are homeless, hungry, and without employment. Others are afflicted with diseases like AIDS, cancer, and diabetes. Artists struggle to find places to perform their works or display their creations. Too many children do not get an adequate education. In many regions of the world the air, land, and water are polluted.

Funders understand that our society has numerous problems and that needs in our communities would often go unaddressed if it were not for the work being done by nonprofit agencies. Although most program officers try to keep abreast of the major social issues, the problems are complex, there is a great deal of information to absorb, and there are only so many hours in the day. We should not expect those individuals reviewing our grant proposals to understand every nuance of every issue. On occasion, they must be educated about the scope and breadth of community needs and problems in order to make informed choices about where to invest their organization's grant dollars. Even if funders thoroughly know of and understand a particular problem or issue, they want you to demonstrate that your agency does too. Program officers expect your agency's staff to be knowledgeable about the field (environment, education, health care, and the like) and the community where the agency provides its services. For these reasons, it is essential for our proposals to thoroughly answer the question, What is the problem or need that's being addressed by the nonprofit agency?

The section of a proposal where this question is answered is known as the problem or needs statement. Using the storytelling approach to grantseeking, this is the proposal section where you lead the reader up the story arc by showing the conflict between main characters and the antagonist. This is absolutely the most important, necessary section in your agency's proposal. Without a specifically defined problem or need, there is simply no reason for the funder to award your agency a grant. And if there is no problem, then there is no reason for your agency even to exist.

It is my observation that novice grantwriters often gloss over or skip altogether this ultra-important section. They assume that funders are already fully informed about a problem or issue. And they do not realize how crucial it is to demonstrate the agency's knowledge. Too often, inexperienced grantwriters are in too big of a hurry to get to the project description or methods section. Yet a good, effective story cannot be rushed. It needs to unfold logically.

HOW LONG SHOULD THE NEEDS SECTION BE?

The proposal reviewer must understand the seriousness and urgency of the problem if he or she is to respond. In this case, responding means making a grant. This is why grantwriters must be articulate and persuasive. Because the problem or need is at the heart of your story, this section should be the lengthiest one in your narrative. How long should it be? In a five-page narrative, the needs section might run a page or a page and a half. A proposal twice as long—say ten pages—would merit a two- to three-page discussion of the need or problem being addressed. Remember, an accomplished author takes the reader on a long ride up the story arc, carefully building the conflict and layering the tension. This lays the foundation for everything else that is to come—namely, the climactic moment and the resolution. Take the proposal reader on a similar journey.

APPLYING THE STORYTELLING METHOD

To write a strong needs or problem statement, grantwriters must be especially articulate, persuasive, and thorough without overstating the problem or being overly dramatic. As a journalism major, I learned the "who, what, when, where, why" method of writing a lead paragraph. This approach applies very well to the drafting of the problem or needs statement. A proposal will have successfully described the problem or need if it has answered the following questions:

- *Who* are the people who have the need or problem?
- *Where* do the people with the problem or need live?
- *When* is the problem or need made evident?
- *Why* does the problem or need occur?
- *What* is the problem with the problem?

Many grantwriters, and you may be among them, find that these questions provide a solid skeleton on which to hang their words and build their narrative. Others may have difficulty applying this framework. In particular, grantwriters sometimes struggle to make sense of the subtle distinctions among the what, when, and why questions. Let me try to help you. My approach is to encourage you to think more like a storyteller when drafting the needs or problem statement. I've found that in doing so you are likely to answer these fundamental questions while weaving together a cohesive and persuasive story.

Presenting the Antagonist

To begin, think about those conditions, circumstances, or forces (collectively, I'll call these societal forces) in your community that are having a negative impact on a segment of the population, namely those people served by your agency. A good example of such a societal force is rampant unemployment and a lack of economic opportunities or jobs in a particular community or neighborhood. Consider the impact of this situation on the people living in this community, which we'll call Central City. When people do not have access to jobs or economic opportunities, there is apt to be poverty, homelessness, and crime. This is a serious situation in need of a response, a solution. Let's consider how the problem can be framed.

- Who are the people with the need, and where do they live? People residing in Central City.

- When is the problem or need made evident? When poverty rates, homelessness, and criminal activity are higher in Central City than in other neighborhoods. Incorporating relevant statistics will help make the case. (This topic is addressed in more detail later in the chapter.)

- Why does the problem or need occur? Obviously, this is a complex question with a complex answer. The lack of educational opportunities (good schools) and employment opportunities (factories, retail businesses, service and technology industries, and so on) are likely factors. A large recent immigrant, non-English-speaking population may be another. A failing infrastructure and an inadequate public transportation system may be additional contributing factors. (Once again, including data will support the case.)

- What is the problem with this problem? One can argue that continuing poverty, homelessness, and crime have higher and more long-term costs than the costs of addressing and trying to fix the problem. There are also human costs in terms of lost opportunities and potential.

There you have it: a needs statement in skeletal form. A skillful writer, armed with more in-depth information and data, can expand on this framework and draft a compelling needs statement.

Now imagine a nonprofit agency working in the economically depressed Central City neighborhood, an agency whose mission is to provide job training and employment skills to community residents. The agency is the hero-protagonist in a proposal narrative facing off against a formidable foe, an antagonist, which is the very serious problem of high unemployment coupled with a lack of employment opportunities. Truly, this makes for a compelling story.

Time to Write!

Have a new request in mind or one that could use some fine-tuning? Create a framework for your need or problem statement by providing brief answers to the following questions:

- Who?
- Where?
- When?
- Why?
- What?

Examples 5.1, 5.2, and 5.3 are three excellent, and very different, illustrations of how to describe the antagonist—the need or problem—in our proposal stories.

Telling the Back Story

Before writing a novel, an author needs to know everything he can about his characters: their strengths, weaknesses, motivations, family backgrounds, education, work experience. All of this information helps define the characters and make them more believable. In fact, some writers even write lengthy biographical sketches about their main characters, including details about their families, friends, and careers.

Example 5.1
The Proposal Antagonist: Describing the Need
in a Child Advocates Proposal

In 2005, 5,500 children in Bexar County were confirmed victims of abuse or neglect, representing nearly 10% of all confirmed child abuse victims in the state. Of these confirmed victims, 1,848 children were removed from their homes and placed in state care. Far from a haven from abuse, the overburdened and under-resourced state care system in many ways revictimizes an intensely vulnerable group of children.

- There are not enough foster homes and other temporary housing facilities for children in care in San Antonio, necessitating that siblings often be separated and placed in homes from blocks to hundreds of miles apart.

- There are not enough Child Protective Services caseworkers to diligently serve each child, ensuring that their needs are met while they are in the system. Even as reform measures are implemented, many CPS caseworkers are carrying up to 80 cases each. There are simply not enough hours in the day for caseworkers to attend to all of the children on their caseload.

- Child abuse legal cases are on the rise. According to Bexar County Courthouse statistics, Bexar County saw 1,416 cases in 2004 up from 884 in 2003—a 60% increase. Minimum requirements for court-appointed attorneys for children do not ensure effective advocacy for each child on these cases.

These factors add up to a painful and scary time for children. Abused and neglected children desperately need an advocate to be a consistent adult presence while they move through the system. They need an advocate to listen to their needs and concerns, to give them a voice in the legal process that determines their futures, and to be there for them as they grieve their losses and vent their frustrations and fears.

Note: This needs statement was written by Jennifer Yeagley, formerly with Child Advocates San Antonio (CASA) and currently the grants manager at LightHouse for the Blind and Visually Impaired, San Francisco.

Example 5.2
Describing the Need for Philanthropy By Design

Philanthropy By Design's (PBD's) work addresses two significant community needs. First, the vast majority of nonprofit agencies in our region do not have the financial resources to make interior improvements and purchase upgraded furnishings. Many agencies make do with drab interior spaces and/or with furniture that is damaged, dingy, or ill suited for its present purpose. For example, it is not unusual for nonprofit agencies to use old and outdated desks that were not designed for computer work and are therefore uncomfortable, and occasionally unsafe, for employees. Nonprofit agencies do not operate effectively and efficiently in such dreary environments. Annually, PBD receives between 30 and 40 requests—and this number is steadily growing—from nonprofit agencies that want our help in improving their interior spaces.

The second need addressed by PBD concerns the environment. Each year, hundreds of Bay Area businesses and hotels update and replace their current furnishings. Others simply close or go out of business. Sometimes unwanted or unneeded furnishings are sold to liquidators, but frequently these items—amounting to hundreds of tons annually—are destined for the landfill. PBD seeks to procure such quality furnishings and recycle them for reuse in local nonprofit agencies. During the past 11 years, PBD has recycled approximately 500 tons of furnishings, placing such items as desks, chairs, tables, sofas, and workstations with community nonprofits.

This material is referred to as the back story, the so-called story behind the story. Much of this back-story material never makes it into the novel itself because its purpose is really to serve the writer. Yet in grantwriting it is important for nonprofit agencies to include back-story information in the proposal. For example, in the problem or needs section, it is essential for the agency to acknowledge other nonprofits in the community that are working to address the same problem. Nonprofits typically don't work in a vacuum. Most likely, other agencies are also working to address the same problem or issue within the same geographic area, and the existence of these other nonprofits should be

Example 5.3
Describing the Need for The Other Bar

A man falls into a hole so deep he can't get out. A doctor walks by, and the man calls for help. The doctor writes a prescription, tosses it into the hole, and walks on. A priest walks by, and the man tries again. The priest writes a prayer, tosses it into the hole, and walks on. Finally a friend walks by, and again the man asks for help. To his surprise, the friend jumps in with him. "Why did you do that?" the man asks. "Now we're both in the hole." "Yes," the friend responds. "But I've been in this hole before, and I know the way out." (anonymous author)

Need for The Other Bar

There is an overwhelming need for assistance for those in the legal profession struggling with alcoholism and drug dependency. The American Bar Association estimates that 15 to 20% of attorneys and judges suffer from alcohol or drug addiction, a rate nearly twice that of the general population. As many as 50 to 70% of the lawyers who are brought before Bar disciplinary committees are chemically dependent. At any one time, approximately 34,000 members of the California State Bar are having problems with alcohol or drugs.

Substance abuse and recovery are difficult for legal professionals and their families. Yet there are others who suffer greatly from impaired lawyers: the clients relying on them. Whether involved in the courts because of civil or criminal matters or seeking private advice about a range of problems (housing, divorce, immigration), clients are victims of alcoholic or drug-addicted lawyers. Their cases may receive insufficient or incompetent attention, deadlines may be missed, and their best outcomes made impossible. Clients may wind up in prison, poor, or without custody of their children because of poor legal service rendered by counsel impaired by alcohol or drug addiction.

It is a failure of the legal profession and of this society's commitment to justice for clients to be victimized by reliance on impaired lawyers. There is a clear public interest in ensuring that lawyers avoid becoming impaired and, if they do succumb, that they get the speediest help with their alcohol or drug problems, so they can be worthy of the trust that their community and their clients place in them.

Note: This excerpt was written by fundraising consultant Judy Kunofsky.

recognized. By doing so, you demonstrate to potential funders that your agency is aware of what is happening in the greater community, and this in turn further demonstrates your agency's credibility.

And because other agencies are working to solve the same problem or unmet community need, your agency's proposal also should explain what specific niche its programs fill. How does its work differ from or complement work being done by other agencies? How is your agency distinguishable from all the others? Perhaps your agency uses different methods to confront the problem and serve clients. Perhaps the agency anticipates achieving different objectives or results. Perhaps it reaches a slightly different segment of the population that otherwise wouldn't be served. Or perhaps the problem is simply so big with so many unserved clients that several agencies in a given community can work on the same issue, each striving to find a solution.

The reason this back-story information is important is that grantmakers want to avoid funding duplicated services. They want to invest their money with agencies that are most likely to have the greatest impact on society. Example 5.4 shows how to acknowledge the work being done by other agencies while promoting your agency's case for support.

Example 5.4
Acknowledging Other
Child Care Centers

Two other early child-care development centers operate in the South of Main Street Area: Little Friends Preschool and St. Bartholomew's Child Care Center. Whereas the South of Main Street Child Care Center (SOMSCC) provides care for infants (as young as three months) and toddlers, Little Friends does not, limiting its enrollment to children ages 3½ to 6. And whereas St. Bartholomew's offers care for infants through preschoolers, it is a much smaller child care center with a total of 45 total spaces compared to SOMSCC's 125. Currently, all three centers have lengthy waitlists (up to two years), particularly for subsidized and scholarship slots at all age levels. This demonstrates the urgent need for more affordable early child care in the South of Main Street Area.

JOINING FORCES WITH OTHER HEROIC AGENCIES

Sometimes a problem, the antagonist, requires the collaborative attention of two or more heroic nonprofit agencies. Collaborations between or among nonprofit agencies have become quite common in recent years. When two or more nonprofit agencies join forces to attack a common foe, the whole is often greater than the sum of the parts. Staff expertise, experience, and other resources combine to bring a more efficient delivery of services. Therefore, collaborations are often encouraged and favored by the grantmaking community. Collaborations provide a means for stretching donated dollars even further, thereby making the funder's investment more worthwhile, as either more clients are reached or those who are reached are better served.

If your agency will partner or collaborate with another nonprofit agency, this is a key element in your proposal story. The teaming of two heroes is always an exciting adventure. Be certain that your narrative captures that excitement. Be specific about each agency's particular role and responsibilities.

USING DATA AND STATISTICS EFFECTIVELY

In describing the problem or need, a judicious use of data and statistics can help strengthen your agency's story by demonstrating the magnitude of the problem. Numbers, graphs, and charts can visually convey mounds of information and put a large exclamation point on the problem. I use the term "judicious" deliberately. Include data and statistics wisely, which usually means sparingly. Forcing the reader to swim through a sea of numbers does little, if anything, to bolster your agency's case. You want to select data that are *relevant*, which means data that are both current and geographically appropriate.

What data to include in a proposal story is a very important consideration, as is substantiating the data. For example, one of my colleagues works for a nonprofit agency whose mission is to eradicate breast cancer; to achieve this mission, the agency provides breast cancer education and advocacy primarily to residents of a particular county. Her agency has volumes of data regarding the incidence of breast cancer. Which ones should she include in a grant proposal?

She could report that 10 percent of females in the United States will be diagnosed with breast cancer during their lifetimes. This is a powerful fact. She has another piece of data: one out of eight women (or 12.5 percent) living in the county served by her agency will be diagnosed with breast cancer. This is another powerful factual statement. If I were to advice her, I would include both statistics in a proposal, assuming both are timely and report current data. The second statistic is geographically relevant because it is specific to the county being served. The first statistic provides a context and highlights the fact that the incidence of breast cancer is even higher in this county than the national average.

Citing Sources, Using Footnotes, and Checking Facts

Sources Always substantiate data included in a proposal by identifying their source. What's a valid source? Primary sources, such as census data and research studies published by reputable institutions, are best. Opinion blogs and tabloid newspapers are not. You always want to cite the best source possible.

Footnotes As a general rule, avoid using footnotes in your proposal stories. Whereas footnotes that cite source materials are acceptable in college papers and theses, they are not in grant proposals. Footnotes are distracting and take the reader out of the narrative flow of the story. Rather than using footnotes, incorporate the source of information and date within the narrative itself. Let me provide you with two options on how to do this. In the first option, the source is included in the sentence with the factual statement; in the second, citation of the source immediately follows the factual statement.

- According to a 2008 study published by the Groverdale Police Department, juvenile crime has increased 22 percent over the past five years in the Riverfront district.
- Juvenile crime has increased 22 percent over the past five years in the Riverfront district. *2008 Report on Neighborhood Crime by the Groverdale Police Department.*

As is true with most "rules," there is usually at least one exception. The exception to the "no footnote" rule in proposals concerns submissions to a very small group of grantmakers, including some federal government agencies and a few large foundations. These funders consider footnotes in proposals to be acceptable. During my career, I have included footnotes in my proposals only a handful of times—when I was absolutely certain that doing so would be in keeping with the funder's institutional culture. In all other circumstances, I have not.

Facts   Don't exaggerate the problem just to make your case. Allow the facts to speak for themselves. Program officers, foundation trustees, and those other folks who review proposals and make funding decisions are intelligent people who will recognize embellishments and inconsistencies when they see them. Program officers may already have expert knowledge of the issue being presented or may undertake their own independent research. If they discover information that contradicts a portion of your agency's story, they are likely to question the validity of the entire proposal. So stick to the straight story. Double-check all your facts. If you do, your agency will be seen as a credible source of information and will have the reader's trust from the proposal's opening paragraph till the closing sentence.

Examples 5.5 and 5.6 do an outstanding job of incorporating relevant data to document the need.

PUTTING A HUMAN FACE ON THE PROBLEM

"A single death is a tragedy; a million deaths is a statistic" is a quote attributed to Soviet dictator Joseph Stalin. Setting aside the unfathomable circumstances that likely preceded his statement, the point he made is well taken. Numbers alone, no matter how outrageous, do not evoke the same emotional response as one strong personal story. For this reason, frequently I will incorporate an anecdote or client story in my proposals.

I include anecdotes when I am reasonably confident that the funder has a favorable opinion of them. In my experience, smaller family foundations and corporate giving programs are receptive to anecdotes and client stories. These funders tend to "give from their hearts." Large institutional funders are not as favorable, for they tend to "give from their heads." Also, funders in different regions of the country seem to respond differently to the inclusion of anecdotes and client stories. Once again, in my experience, grantmakers in the San Francisco Bay Area are more receptive to anecdotes and client stories, whereas grantmakers in other regions are not. The lesson here is: know your funder.

A limited use of anecdotes (one or two) in the narrative serves an important purpose. Anecdotes have the ability to transform a complex societal problem into a very personal one. They also vividly show the impact that an antagonistic societal force can have on a single person, making it more likely that the reader will be able to relate to the issue.

Example 5.5
Documenting the
Community Need in a Planned Parenthood Proposal

For the past five years, teen birthrates have declined in California. Between 1995 and 1996, the rate fell 9% to an average of 58 babies for every 1,000 girls ages 15 to 17. This downward trend proves concretely that funds invested by the government and the private sector in education and prevention programs are indeed working. Yet much work remains to be done.

A 1996 study by University of California researchers and the Center for Health Training identified 82 California communities, "hot spots," where the birthrate for teens is 81 or more per 1,000 teens ages 15 to 17. Planned Parenthood: Shasta Diablo (PPSD) serves three of these communities: Richmond, Vallejo, and Clearlake. PPSD serves other communities, including Concord, Antioch, Pittsburg, Napa, Chico, and Fairfield, where the teen birthrate is significantly above the statewide average.

The consequences for sexually active young women who are not effective contraceptive users are great. Almost half of all teen pregnancies end in birth, slightly more than one-third in abortion, and the rest in miscarriage. The way in which teens resolve their pregnancies is determined largely by their socioeconomic status. Young women from middle-class families generally have abortions. Childbearing, on the other hand, is concentrated among low-income teens; more than 80% decide to have and keep their babies. Only one in ten young mothers is married by the time of the birth of the child, 50% require public assistance to cover medical expenses and subsequent well-baby care, and 30% drop out of high school. Early childbearing has a lasting impact on the lives and future of low-income women and their children.

In addition to the risk of becoming pregnant, young people are contracting HIV and other sexually transmitted infections. Despite a historic drop in AIDS cases and deaths from 1994 to mid-1997, the Centers for Disease Control and Prevention reported that the rate of new infections in young people ages 13 to 24 contracting HIV has not changed.

Note: This excerpt was written by fundraising consultant Laura McCrea and Meike Weyrauch, director of resource development, Planned Parenthood: Shasta Diablo.

Example 5.6
Weaving Data into
a Proposal for Wildlife Preservation

Because no state agency is keeping comprehensive records on poaching activities and enforcement, the exact magnitude of poaching crimes in California is unknown. But statistics collected by the Mountain Lion Foundation show that, far from being isolated incidents, commercial poaching operations have become a multimillion-dollar industry.

The Senate Office of Research estimates that poachers can get $1,000 to $3,000 per ounce for dried and powdered bear gallbladders on the Asian market. Mountain lion gallbladders are indistinguishable from bear gallbladders, so poachers often take both species illegally. Bear paws bring $30 to $100 each. As many as 200 black bears were recently killed by one poaching ring in Redding, California. In Tulare County undercover agents bought $7,000 worth of illegal wildlife hides and parts from poachers, including 55 bobcats, parts of 16 bears, three whole bears, two mountain lions, and dozens of other wildlife. In all, 33 people were arrested and charged for poaching crimes in this one sting operation. Department of Fish and Game personnel agree that arrests for poaching represent only the tip of the iceberg.

Poaching on such a grand scale has a powerful effect on our wildlife and is threatening the very survival of some species. For instance, the number of bears being taken illegally each year in California is at least equal to the number being killed by hunters with permits (700 to 900 in recent years). This potentially represents an annual reduction in the bear population of 12 to 20%. Department of Fish and Game statistics for last year showed that the total deer kill included 64,000 legal kills and an estimated 100,000 illegal kills. Furthermore, a report by the California Department of Parks and Recreation ranked poaching as the third biggest threat to park wildlife.

Note: This example was written by Susan Fox, fundraising consultant and coauthor of *Grant Proposal Makeover: Transform Your Request from No to Yes.*

Create tension in your agency's narrative by describing the challenges and struggles faced by one of your agency's clients. What was life like for the individual before he or she received the services offered by your agency? How has the delivery of such services changed or improved this person's life? By answering these questions, an anecdotal story provides both dramatic tension and hope—hope that the antagonistic force can be confronted and ultimately defeated.

That's because an appropriate anecdote will show the nonprofit agency successfully intervening in the life of a client and thereby making a significant difference. Clearly, the best anecdotes to include in your proposal narratives are stories of client successes. Examples 5.7 and 5.8 illustrate how to do this.

One person's success story stands in stark contrast to the thousands of untold stories of people whose lives have yet to be positively touched by your nonprofit agency. Writing this portion of the proposal narrative is therefore a bit of a

---

Example 5.7
Including a Client Anecdote in a Library Outreach Proposal

Each year, the library's "Books on the Go" program reaches hundreds of individuals, the majority of whom are seniors who cannot leave their homes. So instead of people coming to the library, the library goes to them. Jane is one of the people served by "Books on the Go" last year. Jane is 85 and disabled, living alone and on a fixed income. A former schoolteacher, Jane has been an avid reader all her life. Until a few years ago, Jane used to walk the six blocks to the library almost every week. But then health problems struck, and Jane hasn't been able to get to the library since.

Last year Jane signed up for the "Books on the Go" program. Now Jane is visited monthly by a library volunteer who brings a selection of books for Jane to look through, from which she can choose books to check out till the following month. (To make certain the book selection is appropriate, each participant can indicate the type of books he or she prefers.) Jane is one of the program's most voracious readers, and each month looks forward to seeing the brightly painted "Books on the Go" van pull up outside her home. Jane is not alone. Currently, more than 500 individuals are served by this beloved program.

Example 5.8
Including a Client Anecdote in a Prison Reform Proposal

On August 19, 2005, 19-year-old Joseph Maldonado hanged himself in the CHAD youth prison. Joseph had been in solitary confinement for eight weeks and routinely denied mental health care. An official report concluded that neglect contributed to his death.

On the six-month anniversary of his death, Books Not Bars held a vigil. A month later Joseph's sister, Renee Nuñez, led a No More Lives Lost march on Sacramento. She gave exclusive interviews (arranged by Books Not Bars) to the *Sacramento Bee* and three television stations to tell her story and share memories of Joseph. Next month her op-ed will run in the *LA Times*. In June, she will testify before the state legislature in the confirmation hearing for CYA Chief Bernie Warner.

Without Books Not Bars, there is no outlet for Renee. Her story may emerge, but she could not emerge as a central figure for reform debate.

Note: This excerpt was written by consultant Marie Beichert.

---

balancing act between demonstrating that an urgent need exists and showing the reader that it is possible to meet this need, no matter how great.

GIVING THE LEAD CHARACTERS A VOICE

In most stories, readers get further insight into the characters through dialogue—what the characters actually say and how they say it. Are you aware that you can use dialogue in your proposal stories as well? In grant proposals, client quotes and testimonials serve as the dialogue.

Quotes are especially powerful because through them the proposal reviewer "hears" directly from your agency's clients in their own words. Information is no longer being filtered through your voice as the writer, but instead comes straight from the heart and soul of the people who have been served by the agency. But keep in mind the adage: less is more. Use client quotes and testimonials sparingly. A single eloquent quote that jumps off the page will deliver a greater emotional punch than a series of lackluster quotes.

Examples 5.9 and 5.10 are excerpts from proposals that do their own "talking."

Example 5.9
Incorporating Dialogue: Urban Shakespeare Proposal

The youth served by the Urban Shakespeare program say it best.

- "Urban Shakespeare introduced me to a whole new language I didn't even know existed. Now I love the theater! I especially liked doing the pretend sword fights and death scenes. That was cool," says Jimmy, age 14, who participated in last year's program.

- "I really like Shakespeare. He's a cool dude and a good writer. If he were alive today, he'd be bigger than Stephen King!" says Marissa, age 11, a current participant.

Example 5.10
Client Quotes in a Philanthropy By Design Proposal

From the beginning, Philanthropy By Design (PBD) has filled an important need within the nonprofit community, and our work is deeply appreciated. Here is what two agencies say about PBD: "My agency had no resources to improve the interiors of our buildings, some of which have not been redecorated in 25 to 35 years. PBD's talents and energy are a real blessing for our programs," states Leon Washington, executive director of the Sheffield Center, which provides housing for at-risk youth.

"The assistance provided by PBD is far more significant than just improving a facility's ambiance. An appropriate physical setting is a crucial component of substance abuse treatment. In a very true sense, the work of the PBD team is part of the rehabilitative process when dealing with emotionally troubled youth," says Javier Martinez, Sheffield Center's facilities manager.

WHOSE NEED IS IT ANYWAY?

I want to be absolutely clear about something. The problem or need, the antagonist that I've been discussing, is the one faced by your agency's clients. Their needs are the focal point of a successful grant proposal. A grant proposal is *not* about the needs of the nonprofit agency.

This can be a confusing issue for grantwriters, especially those new to the field, so let me offer some further clarification. Suppose an agency is in need of new capital equipment, specifically new computers. The agency shouldn't seek grant support to purchase new computers by making the case that its staff members will benefit. Instead, the agency should keep the spotlight on the clients—the main characters of its story. The proposal narrative should establish a link between the much-needed computers and the agency's delivery of client services. Would services be improved if staff had faster, more reliable equipment? Would the agency be able to serve more clients thanks to the enhanced capabilities provided by new computers? In a compelling narrative, the answer to both of these questions would be yes. And that's the story to present to potential funders.

PULLING IT ALL TOGETHER

Drafting a compelling need statement is admittedly one of the more challenging tasks for a grantwriter. If you fail to present a worthy need (in other words, if the antagonist is not a believable villain), the reader is apt to have doubts about the validity of the request or to stop reading altogether. I hope I gave you many tips that you'll find useful the next time you sit down to write this section. One final proposal excerpt (Example 5.11 on the next page) does an outstanding job of pulling it all together.

SUMMARY

Here's a brief summary of the key points I covered in the chapter; they will help you present your story's antagonist—that problem or need typically caused by complex societal forces. Your objective is to lead the reader up the story arc by building conflict and tension. You will succeed if you do the following:

- Understand that without a problem or unmet need, there's no reason for your agency to exist or for the grantmaker to provide funding.
- Identify your agency's niche in the community, while acknowledging the work being done by other nonprofit agencies.

Example 5.11
Describing the Need for Petaluma Bounty

Petaluma is a semi-rural city of 56,000 people located at the southern end of Sonoma County. Known for its riverfront setting and Victorian charm, Petaluma is called "gateway to the Wine Country" and is home to several leading organic food processing companies.

Amid the bounty of food on our grocery shelves imported from all over the world, and despite our rich agricultural heritage, Petaluma's food system is leaving many in our community undernourished, unhealthy, and just plain hungry. Although not apparent to the casual observer, there are many families and individuals in Petaluma who do not earn enough to make ends meet and who are suffering the effects of food insecurity and poor nutrition. On May 7, 2006, *The New York Times* reported that this area has the third highest cost of living in the nation, with housing costs eating up 50% or more of many households' monthly income. A growing number of Petaluma families are forced each month to decide between paying rent or buying healthy food:

- More than 20% of children in Petaluma schools are enrolled in free or reduced school meal programs based on their family income levels (many more are eligible, but not enrolled).

- From Summer 2005 to the present, the number of households provided with meals by the Interfaith Pantry (which Petaluma Bounty helped create) has jumped from 16 to almost 100.

- At a recent meeting convened by Petaluma Bounty, each emergency food provider projected continued increases in demand for supplemental food, while noting that the inventory at our local food bank is lower than ever before.

As Sonoma County's wine grape growers and housing developers attempt to meet growing demand for their products, rural land becomes less and less affordable to small-scale vegetable and fruit farmers. Meanwhile, global food conglomerates aggressively market "value-added" food products as much for their entertainment value as for nutrition. Lower-income households are hit the hardest by these forces, experiencing more nutrition-related health problems (such as obesity and type II diabetes) than the rest of the population, and contributing to our overburdened health care system.

Aside from the ever-diminishing nutritional value of much of our food—especially that which is affordable to low-income people—the current food system contributes to serious social and environmental problems, chief among them depletion of topsoil and groundwater pollution from conventional agriculture; loss of small-scale family farms and the critical food and species diversity that such farming supports; fossil-fuel dependence and greenhouse gas emissions from the long-distance transport of food; and loss of local food dollars to distant shareholders who have little investment in our local community.

For Petaluma today, a comprehensive approach to community food security is of paramount importance in the face of the growing number of families facing food insecurity on a daily basis and the many additional unwelcome impacts that this food system brings with it, both locally and globally.

Petaluma is known for creativity, compassion, and considerable resources. The city can boast of strong community involvement, a rich history of cross-institutional partnerships, and a vibrant agricultural heritage. For these reasons, we are confident that we can succeed, even with such an ambitious program.

Note: This example was written by fundraising consultant Judy Kunofsky.

- Use relevant data and statistical information judiciously to strengthen your case for support. Data are relevant when they are current and geographically relevant.

- Cite the sources of all data within the narrative itself and avoid (in most circumstances) using footnotes.

- Give the problem a human face by incorporating one or two anecdotes in your proposal when appropriate.

- Use client quotes and testimonials as the dialogue in your proposal story.

- Write about clients' problems or unmet needs, not the agency's.

Goals, Objectives, and Methods

Making Changes by Addressing the Problem

G un shots ring out. Or lovers, long separated, arrive at the chosen time and destination. Or perhaps a young girl's hand reaches into an empty space under the floorboard.

Each of these incidents would be a gripping moment in a story because something significant, something climactic, is about to happen. Something will change the lives of the main characters forever. What happens next? What will change? The job of the storyteller is to provide the answers.

Similarly, a proposal story isn't finished until it too has reached a climactic moment and the reader's questions about what will happen next have been answered.

THE GOALS AND OBJECTIVES SECTION

The problem or needs section of a proposal describes the unmet needs of or problems faced by the story's main characters, the agency's clients. The hero agency must intervene and provide effective services. By doing so, the societal problem can be addressed. The unmet need can be fulfilled. The lives of the agency's clients can be improved.

What follows the needs section in the proposal narrative is a discussion about what changes are possible if the nonprofit agency secures the necessary grant funding, allowing it to respond to the problem and deliver vital services.

Because such change is prospective, this section is also prospective. When writing this section of the proposal, grantseekers are like sci-fi writers who envision the future. Of course, there is one critical difference: whereas sci-fi writers present fantasy, grantwriters discuss what is realistic and feasible.

To understand this concept, it may help to think in visual terms. Take a mental snapshot of the community where your nonprofit agency does its work today, at this very moment. What is the problem or unmet need that your agency addresses? Who are the people served by your agency? What more could your agency do if it had additional funds?

Now imagine taking a second mental photograph of this same community at the end of the projected grant period. Compare it with the earlier snapshot. What's different? How has the need been met? How have the clients been served? Most important, how have the lives of your agency's clients been altered and positively changed? You should "see" a noticeable difference between these two mental snapshots. (If you don't, then perhaps your agency's services aren't as effective as they could be.)

How the community and your story's main characters (your agency's clients) will have changed is portrayed in the goals and objectives section of a grant proposal. The challenge in writing this portion of your proposal story is to vividly and accurately describe to the reader the change(s) that will take place, as represented by those two mental snapshots. The change that occurs helps reduce or resolve the conflict (the problem or need).

Readers appreciate a story that has a believable, satisfying resolution. Program officers and others reviewing grant proposals do too. The validity of your request hinges on whether the resolution of the conflict rings true. If it doesn't, the story falls flat and short of the mark, no matter how well it is written or told.

The Difference Between Goals and Objectives

It is typical for funders to ask applicants for a description of agency goals and objectives in the proposal narrative. Many people confuse these terms: goal and objective. I confess to having been confused myself early in my grantwriting career. So just what is a goal? What is an objective? And how do they differ?

Goals A *goal* is the ultimate result an agency hopes to achieve. Goals are big and broad. A goal is unlikely to be accomplished in the near future. In fact, arriving at an agency's end goal could be years or even decades away. It is possible that the end goal will never be achieved. A small or medium-size nonprofit agency is likely to have only one or two, or perhaps up to three, primary goals. If your agency thinks it has more goals than that, then it may be in danger of being unfocused and trying to accomplish too much. Or the agency may be confusing goals with objectives or outcomes.

Large, complex nonprofit agencies, such as universities, hospitals, and leading cultural arts institutions, are the exception and are likely to have dozens, perhaps hundreds, of legitimate goals. For example, a major research university will have many institution-wide goals, and each of its dozens of departments (from theater arts to biotechnology) will have dozens of departmental goals.

Expressing agency-wide, departmental, or program goals can be challenging, especially when you or other agency staff haven't thought in these terms before. To help you, here are some examples of "big picture" agency and program goals:

Agency-Wide Goals

- End hunger in Center City
- Find a cure for breast cancer
- Save the black rhinoceros from extinction

Program-Specific Goals

- Provide arts education to every elementary school child in the Yuma Valley School District
- Provide free legal services to every indigent client who walks through our doors

Objectives   In contrast to goals, *objectives* are capable of being achieved in the short term. People sometimes think of objectives as "mini-goals." To add to the confusion, funders may refer to objectives using other terms, such as outcomes or results. For consistency, I will continue to use *objectives* throughout the book.

For each overall goal, there can be one or more related objectives. It would be highly unusual to have six or more objectives related to any one goal. When I read a proposal with that many stated objectives, what I often discover is that the writer has confused objectives with methods. I will say more about this topic later in the chapter.

Objectives are realistic. They state what is most likely going to happen. They are time specific, meaning that change is measured during a specific period, which typically coincides with the grant period. The strongest objectives are also capable of being measured. (One exception is with proposals for the arts. It is difficult, if not impossible, to measure the impact of a dance performance on the audience. However, audience attendance is capable of being measured.)

Typically, objectives measure the change that happens in your agency's client population during the grant period. Something is going to improve because of the services offered by your agency. Something is going to increase, decrease, expand, or be reduced. This change is generally reported in terms of percentages or numbers.

Is this all sounding too vague and confusing? I think a couple of examples may help.

Suppose an agency runs a teen pregnancy prevention program. The agency's overall goal might be stated as follows:

Because every child deserves to be wanted, our goal is to eliminate all unwanted teen pregnancies in our community.

This is a goal because it is an end result the agency hopes to accomplish, though it is not likely to do so in the immediate future. This statement is not an objective because it cannot be measured and is not realistic (at least not in the short term). However, the following are objectives that relate back to the agency's overall goal:

- To *increase* the number of teens participating in our agency's peer education program by 30 percent
- To achieve a 25 percent *decrease* in teen pregnancies in the next academic year at the two high schools participating in our agency's peer education program

If you're still unclear, let these concepts percolate for a time. From talking with a number of people who have taken my workshops, especially people new to the grantseeking field, I have learned that understanding goals and objectives is one of the most challenging aspects of proposal writing. It is a concept that is frequently best understood over time. Be patient. Review examples in other grant proposals. There are several examples presented in this book. In addition, read proposals written by other agency staff or colleagues working for other agencies. If you want to be a better writer, the best advice is summarized by three words: read, read, read.

Your Agency as Hero, Not Superhero: Keeping Objectives Realistic

How do goals and objectives fit into the storytelling metaphor? Here's how. In the best stories, the characters don't do anything that isn't believable, especially at the climactic, pivotal moment. If the characters act otherwise, the storyteller risks losing the audience's trust and interest. This is also true in proposal writing.

To stay with this metaphor, nonprofit agencies should present themselves as heroes, not superheroes, in proposal narratives. Nonprofits can do and achieve the possible, not the impossible. Your nonprofit agency probably will not be able to save the planet. But it can do something. What your agency does is much more realistic than "saving the planet": its delivery of services has a positive impact on people living in the community—pretty heroic work in its own right. When developing objectives, keep them realistic. This is advice that you, as grantwriter, may need to give to your agency colleagues, particularly program directors. Sometimes they believe that objectives need to be large in order to impress potential grantmakers. Yet this is not the case.

What are realistic objectives? The answer to this question varies considerably from agency to agency and from program to program. What's realistic depends on several factors. These include, but certainly are not limited to, the complexity of the identified problem, the maturity of the program and how long it has been in existence, the specific nature of the agency's response to the problem, the receptiveness of its clients to the agency's response, and the experience and expertise of agency staff. In some situations, a 5 percent positive change would be considered terrific. Under other conditions, a respectable figure might be 15 or 25 percent. In others, an appropriate number may be something approaching 100 percent. It all depends on what is truly realistic and feasible given all the circumstances.

However, stating that your nonprofit agency will be able to double its service capacity or effect a 100 percent positive transformation for its clients is likely to raise a funder's eyebrow. At first blush, this appears to be a huge change. A program officer most certainly will wonder, "Is this objective possible? Is it realistic?"

It is, of course, not theoretically impossible for a nonprofit agency to substantially increase its services during the relatively short one-year grant period. (Yes, I used a double negative. I'm trying to make a point about just how unlikely it is for such dramatic changes or improvements to be made in any given time frame. Most often, real transformation occurs slowly over time.) If your agency thinks it has the capacity to significantly increase its delivery of services, your proposal story must thoroughly explain how this will happen.

Similarly, if your agency anticipates that it can effect a near-perfect result—say in the graduation rate of participating clients—then the narrative must clearly demonstrate why this is likely. Staying with the program graduation example, it is rare for everyone who begins a program to remain in the program for the duration and finish. People drop out for a variety of reasons. Why will your program be different? What does it offer people that motivates them to stay to the end?

To summarize, the goals and objectives section is the climactic moment in your proposal story. This is the moment when lives are changed—in many situations, forever.

Length and Format of the Goals and Objectives Section

The goals and objectives portion of a proposal is usually one of the lengthier sections. In our hypothetical five-page proposal narrative, a discussion of goals and objectives could easily run a full page, and in a ten-page narrative, this section may run two to three pages. Together with the needs or problem statement, this is the core of your proposal story.

When it comes to formatting this portion of the proposal, you may want to consider using bulleted lists rather than narrative prose. Using bullets is an acceptable option. Bulleted lists help organize dense or complicated materials.

Examples 6.1, 6.2, and 6.3 are three proposal excerpts that illustrate the goals and objectives section.

THE METHODS SECTION

In mountain climbing, getting to the top of the peak is only half the journey. Successfully returning to base camp is just as important as the ascent. The same is true with a story. A storyteller leads the reader on a journey up the story arc to the pivotal moment, and then just as deliberately guides the reader back down. Following the proposal story's climactic moment, there's still more action. What comes next is the methods section.

The methods section (which may be called the program description) of a proposal describes all the strategies and activities your agency will use, the personnel who will be employed, and the other resources that will be marshaled in order to achieve the objectives stated in the proposal. Methods present your agency's plan of action.

Be careful not to confuse methods with objectives. Methods describe what the agency will do to achieve stated objectives. Objectives describe the change that

---
Example 6.1
Outcomes for a Child Advocates Program

During the grant period, the recruitment and retention efforts of our Volunteer Coordinator will allow 260 volunteers to serve 1,327 children. Additionally, we will achieve the following outcomes:

- 97% of the children we serve will have one volunteer advocate throughout the duration of their case, providing constancy and consistency at an otherwise unstable time.

- 92% of the children we serve will be impacted specifically because of the work of the volunteer advocate.

- 98% of the time the judge will agree with CASA's recommendation for a safe and permanent home for the children we serve.

Note: This excerpt was written by Jennifer Yeagley, formerly with Child Advocates San Antonio (CASA) and currently the grants manager at LightHouse for the Blind and Visually Impaired, San Francisco.

---

will occur. For example, "Provide on-site after-school tutoring for twenty middle school students during the winter term" is a method. "Academically, sixteen of the twenty students (80 percent) will improve at least one letter grade (for example, from a D to a C or from a C to a B) by the end of term" is an objective.

The temptation among grantwriters is to slide right past objectives and begin describing methods. To have a strong proposal, you must resist temptation. Make certain you have articulated realistic, measurable objectives before you launch into a description of the program.

How Much Detail to Include in the Methods Section

As just mentioned, the vast majority of grantwriters feel comfortable writing the methods portion of a proposal. They are generally very knowledgeable about how the agency goes about doing its work and providing its services. One of the challenges in doing a good job with this section is knowing just how much detail to include.

Example 6.2

Goals and Outcomes for the GRIP/Rubicon Resource Center

The goal of the GRIP/Rubicon Resource Center is to help homeless West County families stabilize their lives so that they can find permanent solutions to their housing needs. This goal is directly aligned with United Way's funding priority #10 for Contra Costa County: to enable the homeless and those with special needs to obtain appropriate housing. Outcomes to be achieved by the resource center are as follows.

Intermediate Outcomes

- 400 unduplicated individuals will be linked with temporary housing and other services each year.

- 170 adults will commit to partnership agreements, and 102 (60%) will find transitional or permanent housing each year.

Long-Term Outcomes

- Out of 102 individuals who find transitional or permanent housing through the program each year, 71 (70%) will remain in permanent housing for one full year.

Note: This excerpt was written by fundraising consultant Susan Fox, coauthor of *Grant Proposal Makeover: Transform Your Request from No to Yes.*

Savvy storytellers do not bog down their stories with lots of mundane details. They selectively include only the most pertinent facts that move the story forward. Do the same in your grant proposals. Funders want you to describe the key elements and components of a program, but not the minutia. Here's an example. Suppose you work for a nonprofit educational organization that provides vocation and career training for adult students. In a proposal narrative, it is important for you to tell the funder that your agency is committed to teaching in a classroom setting rather than offering students online learning. It is also appropriate to state that classes are offered evenings and weekends to best accommodate its primary

---

Example 6.3
Program Goals and Objectives for New Door Ventures

Program Goals

During the one-year funding period, we expect to employ 40 high-risk, transitional youth in this program. We will provide case management; life, academic, and employment skills training; mentoring; and supportive services to all program participants.

Program Outcomes

The key outcomes of our program are as follows:

- 85% of participants will successfully graduate from the six-month internship program.

- 85% of the program graduates will successfully transition into mainstream jobs and/or be enrolled in school.

- 90% of graduates will live in stable housing upon graduation.

Note: This excerpt was written by grantwriting consultant Carol Lena Figueiredo.

---

student population, namely adults working full-time. However, it is not necessary to include information about what color binders are used for the school's handout materials, or the names of the specific textbooks used in courses. This latter information is irrelevant minutia.

Time to Write!

Let's see if the concepts presented in this chapter have had time to fully percolate. I'm going to ask you to write one overall goal for your agency or one of its major programs and at least one related objective (outcome or result) your agency or program plans to achieve in the coming year. Hint for success: your objective will be stronger if it is capable of being measured and it is realistic.

Funders generally prefer a "bigger picture" description of your program. They are more likely to be interested in understanding the rationale for why your agency selected the method(s) it has chosen. Continuing with the vocational school example, it is probably appropriate that your proposal include a discussion as to why it has chosen to meet the needs of adult students with classroom learning versus online learning. What are the benefits to the students? To the school? What research, if any, did your institution undertake to reach its conclusion?

Here are some of the broader questions to consider when thinking about your agency's rationale for the method(s) it has selected:

- Is your agency continuing an existing program because it has proven to be successful?

- Is your agency enhancing and improving an existing program? If so, what are those enhancements and improvements?

- Is your agency adopting methodology that has been successfully used by other nonprofits elsewhere?

- Is your agency pioneering new methods or developing a pilot program that can be replicated by other agencies?

Tips About Timelines and Bulleted Lists

Your work in drafting the methods section will be made easier if your agency has prepared a detailed timeline for the proposed program. A timeline will assist you and other agency personnel in identifying all those tasks and activities that need to take place during the grant period in order to achieve agency objectives. One of the benefits of having a timeline is that it will help you remember all the steps involved when the time comes to write the proposal. A timeline is usually an internal working document for the grantwriter and other agency staff members. On occasion, some grantmakers ask applicants to include a timeline with the proposal package. If they do, I usually provide one that is less detailed than the version used internally by the agency.

When presenting your program description, you may want to organize this information by a specific time period (for example, by months or quarters) in a bulleted-list format. This can help with clarity and readability.

Another formatting option is to group objectives with corresponding methods. Here's an example for a program called Just Jobs.

Objective 1

• To successfully place in full- or part-time employment 70 percent of the youth who complete the six-month Just Jobs program

Methods

• During the first quarter, program staff will meet with each participant at least four times to determine skills, experience, aptitude, and individual interests by using interview techniques as well as skills and aptitude tests.

• Concurrently with individual meetings, staff will also conduct group workshops and training sessions on the job search process.

• Beginning in the second quarter, program staff will research job opportunities and create a job board that lists appropriate employment opportunities for youth in the community.

• Also beginning in the second quarter, program staff will start contacting local employers, providing them with information about the Just Jobs program. Staff intends to do an introductory mailing to local employers, which will then be followed up with personal telephone calls.

Time to Write!

To sharpen your focus when writing the methods portion of a proposal, write down the three to five key elements that differentiate your program from others.

Program Promises

Other than the common pitfalls I've mentioned previously, drafting the program description or methods is usually not one of the sections that gives grantwriters difficulty. Think of the methods as the promise of what your agency will do to assist clients. Examples 6.4 and 6.5 are excerpts from agencies that wrote their promises exceptionally well.

Example 6.4
Methods in a Philanthropy By Design Proposal

Recommendations about which design projects to undertake are made by a Philanthropy By Design (PBD) committee composed of volunteer architects and interior designers, following site visits to the nonprofit agencies that request our help. PBD's board of directors reviews these recommendations and makes the final decision.

Once a project is selected, volunteers such as architects, designers, manufacturing professionals, and members of the general public work under a project manager to complete the job. Each project team works closely with the client agency to determine the exact scope of work and to set a realistic timeline.

PBD asks each client agency to pay a modest fee that ranges from $100 to $500, depending on the size of the project. When possible, PBD also requests agency involvement in the hands-on work of the project. For example, clients of the nonprofit agency and PBD volunteers frequently work side by side on "paint days." Involving those who will actually benefit from an improved facility (such as residents in transitional housing) helps ensure that the new furnishings and enhanced environment will be respected and maintained.

Example 6.5
Methods in a School Readiness and Family Literacy Program

Our school readiness and family literacy program serves 25 preschool children, all low income and all receiving government assistance. Families are Latino/Hispanic, and English is not their primary language. Our program is modeled after one pioneered by the Caridad Children's Center. It is designed to fully integrate early childhood education with culturally appropriate parent support and adult education. First, we evaluate each family's literacy needs. Working together, our staff and participating parents and guardians create a mutually agreed-on action plan. Plans may include parent enrollment in ESL classes, family participation in our "Raising a Reader" program, and parent attendance at workshops we will offer throughout the year. Our bilingual staff will meet with parents periodically during the year to assess how the plan is working and to discuss their child's progress.

SUMMARY

A proposal story builds to the point where something is about to happen. That something is the objectives or outcomes the agency intends to achieve through the services it provides. In this chapter, I covered two major sections in any grant proposal: goals and objectives and methods. When drafting these components, keep the following in mind:

- Think broad (goals) and narrow (objectives).
- Think prospectively. Objectives and methods describe what your agency intends to make happen and how during the grant period.
- Take a mental photograph of the community served by your agency, before and after the grant. Objectives measure the change that occurs to this client population between the beginning and the end of the grant period.
- Keep your intended results realistic and measurable.
- Focus on the bigger picture in the program description: key elements and rationale for choosing the method(s), not minutia.

Evaluation and Future Funding

Writing the Epilogue and Planning for a Sequel

By this point in the proposal, you've thoroughly engaged the reader with your story. The reader is acquainted with the characters and understands the problem. The drama has unfolded, and a resolution has been suggested. But what happens next? Assuming the request is funded, how will the funder, and the agency, know whether or not the program actually was successful? Were the clients adequately served? Did the projected changes occur? Furthermore, once a specific grant ends, are there additional sources of available funding enabling the program to continue? To answer these important questions, grantwriters must include both an epilogue (a discussion about how the program will be evaluated) and plans for a sequel (a section on how the program will be funded in the future) in their proposal stories.

THE EPILOGUE AND WHY IT'S IMPORTANT

When we read a book, we make an investment of time. If the story is a good one, it was time well spent, and we don't feel cheated. But if the story turns out to be a disappointment, we've lost something valuable and precious to most of us: our time. And if we purchased the book, we're also out a few bucks.

Consider the grant proposal. Whenever a proposal is submitted to a potential grantmaker, someone (a program officer, trustee, or other reviewer) also invests time to read and review the submission. If the funder decides to fund the proposal, the institution makes a monetary investment as well, one that is certainly a great deal larger than the cost of a book. To make better funding decisions, grantmakers want to understand how the nonprofit agency will assess a proposed program for its effectiveness.

Therefore, the epilogue portion of a grant proposal describes how the nonprofit agency will assess whether it achieved its stated objectives and followed its proposed methods. Including this information in your proposal demonstrates to the grantmaker that your agency truly cares, just as the funder does, about the clients it serves. By evaluating the effectiveness of its programs, your agency also learns what works and what does not. With this information, the agency can make improvements to the program in the years following the grant period. Ideally, this will result in better delivery of its services and achievement of its objectives.

Remember, the evaluation or assessment process takes place after the grant is awarded and during the implementation phase of the program. It is a wise course of action for a nonprofit agency to incorporate evaluation planning into its program planning. I want to emphasize this point. The time to think about the information an agency wants to gather and how it will go about gathering it is upon the inception of a new program. Yet too many agencies don't consider these issues until the program is up and running—sometimes for many years. What often happens then is that a potential funder asks serious questions about the agency's past performance and its evaluation process that the agency cannot answer. This creates much internal panic, and sometimes the loss of potential funding, which could have been avoided had the agency done some earlier planning.

The task of determining the appropriate evaluation strategies and methods is customarily handled by the program director, the executive director, or both. As a grantwriter, you may play a key role in reminding staff colleagues about the importance of evaluation to funders and guiding them during the decision-making process.

EVALUATION TOOLS, STRATEGIES, AND REPORTS

Evaluation tools are many and varied. They can be quantitative (relying on statistics and data) or qualitative (assessing the experience and feelings of the people who received the agency's services). Often agencies will use a combination of both quantitative measures and qualitative assessments when undertaking an evaluation of programs. Among the many assessment tools at your agency's disposal are observation, questionnaires, surveys, focus groups, one-on-one interviews, pretests and posttests, and intake and exit interviews. Decisions regarding what evaluation tools to use are based on the complexity and comprehensiveness of the program, the information being sought, and the costs involved.

When evaluating large, complex, and high-cost programs, agencies are likely to hire outside evaluators, professionals who can design and implement the process. For smaller, simpler, and less costly programs, it is frequently more appropriate and economical to use in-house personnel and resources. The evaluation process itself may be ongoing throughout the duration of the program, or assessment may need to take place only when certain benchmarks are reached or particular events occur.

The financial investment for an evaluation may be minimal or may represent a significant portion of a program's budget. Generally, the larger, more complex, and more expensive the program, the more detailed and costly the evaluation process will be. This should be kept in mind when an agency is developing its program budget. In recent years, with grantmakers continuing to emphasize the importance of evaluation, more funders are receptive to considering funding all or a portion of the evaluation costs. Some funders have gone so far as to require applicants to include evaluation costs in the program budget. And it is common to see evaluation costs as a line item in the budget forms for government grant applications.

In your proposal, explain the agency's rationale for its choice of assessment tools. This decision may depend a great deal on your agency's available financial and staff resources. Grantmakers usually are more interested in evaluation strategies that assess whether the objectives were met than in those assessing whether the agency's proposed methods were followed. Therefore, the evaluation section, like the rest of the proposal narrative, should focus on the story's main characters—the agency's clients—and how their lives will be improved.

It is equally important to tell the funder how your agency intends to use the assessment information in the future. Presumably, data and materials will be gathered, compiled, analyzed, and finally summarized in a written report, which will be distributed to the appropriate individuals, such as senior staff, board members, and possibly others outside the agency. Some grantmakers make it a condition of their grants that they receive a written report at the end of the funding period. But even if a funder doesn't request a full-blown report, it is proper etiquette to deliver to all funders a brief written summary or letter at the end of the grant period.

This section of your proposal needn't be lengthy. In our hypothetical five-page narrative, a paragraph or two will do.

HOW TO WRITE A COMPELLING EVALUATION SECTION

Far from being dull, the evaluation section—this epilogue-like portion of the proposal—can be as creatively written as the rest of the proposal. In one sense, an assessment can be viewed as a dialogue between the hero (the agency) and the main characters (its clients). The conversation concerns how well agency services are meeting expectations and addressing needs. The evaluation component of a proposal forecasts how frequently that dialogue will take place and under what conditions.

Examples 7.1, 7.2, and 7.3 are strong illustrations of what I mean.

Example 7.1
Evaluation for an Early Child Development Program

An annual evaluation of our program is conducted using (1) the Thelma Harms Environmental Rating Scales for Infants and Children and (2) the family questionnaire developed by the California Department of Education (CDE). Parents participate in both evaluations, as well as in the organization improvement plan that is submitted annually to the CDE. During the year, parents are also involved with our staff in implementing the program improvement plan. The children themselves, especially our toddlers and preschoolers, have input into our curriculum and activities through their identified interests. We use the CDE Desired Results Instrument to assess each child within two months of entry into our program and every three to six months thereafter depending on the age of the child. Our staff and administration interpret the results, and these assist in program planning.

Example 7.2
Evaluation by Shakespeare at Stinson

Shakespeare at Stinson programs are evaluated by our patrons through audience surveys, by participants in special programs (such as the apprenticeship program), and from time to time by outside theater professionals and other community organizations.

Students participating in the apprenticeship program are interviewed at the end of their tenure by one of the teachers who recommended them for the program and by at least one member of our artistic staff. Students are also required to write a thorough evaluation of the program and describe at length what their learning experience has been.

As part of our ongoing evaluation, we contact local teachers and school districts on a regular basis to discuss how we might improve our outreach programs.

Note: This excerpt was written by fundraising consultant Marian Breeze.

Example 7.3
Measuring the Success of the Ridge, Kids and Stewards Program

Currently, program facilitators administer both a pretest and a posttest to youth participants in order to measure what information is learned by the students during the six-week program. At the conclusion of each session, we also ask participating teachers to complete a detailed evaluation questionnaire so we can continue to find ways to improve an already excellent program.

The Ridge, Kids and Stewards (RKS) program is also regularly evaluated by an outside panel of professional evaluators. Because it is our goal to teach young people to become stewards of the environment, the RKS program coordinator and others are working to develop a more sophisticated, yet practical, evaluation process in order to measure the long-term impact of the program on youth who participate.

Time to Write!

Please take a few minutes to jot down your answers to the following questions:

- Who evaluates your programs? Be specific.
- What tools are used to evaluate your programs? Once again, be specific.
- How frequently do evaluations occur? Are they ongoing, or are they triggered by certain benchmark events?
- Who analyzes the compiled data?
- Who receives copies of the evaluation report?

THE SEQUEL AND WHY IT'S IMPORTANT

When an author excels at creating a book that thoroughly captures the public's admiration, there are usually calls for a sequel. As readers, we become so attached to the principal characters in a marvelous story that we yearn for their adventures to continue. Sometimes authors plan on writing a sequel, or even a book series, from the moment a story idea is conceived. (Think Harry Potter.) Other times, upon completing a book, a sequel just seems like the right thing to do. I don't know when author Frank McCourt decided to pen a sequel to *Angela's Ashes*, but wasn't it clever of him to end that award-winning book with the word that became the title of its sequel, *'Tis*? That he hints at a sequel in the final chapter is a stroke of genius.

Naturally, my discussion of sequels has a parallel in the world of grantseeking. The years immediately following the grant period are the sequel to your agency's story as told in the grant proposal. What happens after specific grant funding ends is tremendously important to the funder that makes the grant. Before a funder commits to making a financial investment in your agency, the funder has a strong vested interest in knowing that the program is sustainable. A funder wants reasonable assurance that your agency and its programs will continue and that clients will continue to be served well into the future. If the funder doesn't receive at least some assurances regarding the sustainability of your agency and its programs, then why would it choose to invest in your agency in the first place?

Because grantmakers want to see your agency's story continue, grantwriters have no choice but to prepare for a sequel, which is why every grant proposal should include a section on future funding.

WHY YOU NEED A FUTURE FUNDING PLAN

There will be no sequel for your agency and its programs unless it has a plan in place for securing funding in the future. In the proposal narrative, describe the strategy your agency will undertake to secure this funding. This need not be a lengthy section. Returning to our hypothetical five-page proposal, one or two paragraphs will suffice.

The first rule in preparing for the sequel is never, ever to assume that a grantmaker will renew a grant indefinitely. Nonprofit agencies should always prepare for the day when a funder, no matter how supportive and generous, ceases its support. There are many valid reasons why grantmakers will stop funding a particular agency at some point.

Numerous corporations and foundations state in their guidelines whether or not a grantee can seek renewed funding and, if so, for how long. Some funders may also require a grantee to "take a break" after it has received continuous support for a certain number of years. For example, a foundation may limit grantees to three consecutive years of funding, after which the agency cannot reapply for at least a year.

Another reason why seemingly predictable grant funding may stop is that grantmakers periodically change their funding priorities, and a previously funded agency may discover that it no longer fits within the funder's guidelines. Finally, although it may be disappointing, the agency itself may simply cease being competitive for the limited financial resources available from a particular grantmaker.

For all these reasons, do not assume that once the grant faucet has been turned on, it will stay on.

THE FUTURE FUNDING SECTION

A well-conceived future funding section gives the funder a solid blueprint detailing how the nonprofit agency intends to raise money in order to continue operating its programs and meeting the needs of people in the community. A statement like the following is woefully inadequate: "In subsequent years, St. Joseph's Hospital will fund the Healthy Heart Project from a variety of sources." The future funding section must be much more specific.

What funding strategies can a nonprofit agency employ to secure its future and that of its programs? Here's a list of popular and practical funding strategies:

- *Fee for service.* Consider whether it is appropriate for your nonprofit agency to charge clients a fee (either a flat rate or on a sliding scale) for its services.

- *Entrepreneurial business ventures.* Borrow strategies from the for-profit world. Revenue can be generated from thrift shops, retail stores, and coffee stands, and from the sale of greeting cards, CDs, videos, and other merchandise.

- *Membership program or annual fund campaign.* Think about targeting individual donors by implementing a membership program or an annual fund campaign (or both) to reach more individual donors. If your agency already has these programs in place, are there ways to increase their fundraising potential?

- *Major-gifts program.* Consider building a major-donor program by identifying, cultivating, and soliciting donors with the potential to make large gifts.

- *New donor acquisition program.* Explore starting a direct-mail acquisition program to add new donors.

- *The Internet.* If your agency hasn't already done so, consider providing opportunities for donors to make online donations to your agency.

- *Corporate sponsorships.* Consider whether your agency should partner with corporate and business sponsors, especially when seeking funding for such events as galas, golf tournaments, and the like.

- *Employer-based fundraising.* Think about qualifying your agency to participate in employer-based fundraising campaigns, such as the United Way and federated campaigns.

- *Government funding.* Research whether local, state, or federal agencies provide funding for programs run by your agency.

- *Grantseeking.* Conduct research to identify new potential grantmakers and write more proposals!

Any of these activities—and perhaps you can think of additional ones—may prove to be effective fundraising strategies for covering the costs of your nonprofit agency's future work. In a proposal narrative, describe with as much specificity as possible which of these strategies your agency will use. If a specific strategy involves hiring additional staff or independent contractors, mention this as well. For example, if your agency has budgeted the funds to hire a major gifts officer or retain the services of a contract grantwriter in order to increase funding from those respective areas, tell the funder. This demonstrates a commitment on your agency's part to raising the funds necessary to sustain its programs in the future.

There are consequences if a nonprofit agency cannot fund its future work: a community problem or unmet need goes unaddressed. As a result, people (clients) are negatively affected. Like the main characters in a "good read," these are people whose welfare the grantmaker cares deeply about. Funders want assurances that these people will continue to be served in the years to come. Make sure your proposal provides this assurance in the future funding section.

Admittedly, the future funding section is not the flashiest portion of a grant proposal. But it is a very important section to a potential grantmaker. Continue to use an energetic, positive writing style. Select lively, dynamic words. Have a definite strategy. Be honest and realistic. And you will compose a thorough and engaging future funding section.

I have two examples to share with you (see Examples 7.4 and 7.5).

Example 7.4
Future Funding for LightHouse for the Blind and Visually Impaired

---

LightHouse for the Blind and Visually Impaired is committed to ensuring the continuance of the deaf-blind Enchanted Hills Camp (EHC) session and has been offering it for more than 30 years. Expansion of EHC outreach into the East Bay, specifically targeting prospective campers under the age of 55, will broaden our service network and access to additional funding specific to this geographic area (such as the East Bay Community Foundation). We will pursue new public and private grant streams, as well as contributions from individuals, to maintain this project's momentum. Additionally, we will maintain strong collaborative relationships with our partners, providing strong oversight of deaf-blind services and EHC and continue to execute prudent fiscal oversight of all operations to ensure the EHC deaf-blind session is operating efficiently and, thus, in a sustainable way.

Note: This excerpt was written by Jennifer Yeagley, grants manager for LightHouse for the Blind and Visually Impaired, San Francisco.

Time to Write!

In ten words or less, write your agency's future funding strategy. Think it can't be done? Here's an example:

- Hire consultant

- Train board

- Solicit major gifts

- Expand donor base

Once you have these pithy forecasting statements, you can convert them to a longer version of your agency's future funding plan.

SUMMARY

A good story leaves the reader wanting more. A riveting grant proposal does the same. This is why successful grant proposals include an epilogue and a sequel. The epilogue is the evaluation section, and the sequel is about future funding.

You'll write stronger epilogues and sequels if you remember the following points from this chapter:

- Keep in mind that an evaluation assesses whether the nonprofit agency achieved its stated objectives and followed its proposed methods.

- State why your agency selected the assessment techniques that it did. Determining factors include the size and complexity of the program as well as what resources, time, personnel, and financial resources the agency has available.

- Consider whether it is appropriate to include evaluation costs in the program budget.

- Tell the funder how your agency plans to sustain its work in the future. Funders that make a financial investment in an agency want reasonable assurances that work begun under a grant will continue after the grant period ends.

- Never assume that grant funding from a particular source will continue indefinitely; your agency must plan today for its financial future.

The Budget

Translating Your Story from Words to Numbers

One of the most essential components of a grant proposal is not even written in words. It is the all-important budget. A budget is really nothing more than the translation of your agency's narrative story into another language, the language of numbers. Just as some of us jump to the end of a book to read the ending first, some funders will begin their review of your proposal story by looking at the budget. Eventually, all funders will spend considerable time reviewing the budget, so you need to take care when preparing it.

If you are not an accountant or an MBA, the numbers portion of a proposal can seem especially intimidating, frustrating, and confusing. But like them or not, numbers are a critical part of your agency's story. So don't skip this chapter just because you think numbers are boring, difficult to get a handle on, or too painful to deal with. Your agency's program budget is a necessary and critical element of the proposal story, as are the agency's financial statements, for they complement and strengthen the narrative itself.

WHO TRANSLATES THE NARRATIVE TO NUMBERS?

Although this book's storytelling theme and the translation metaphor apply nicely to this chapter's discussion on budgets, there is one minor wrinkle. When books and stories are translated from English into another language, the author

113

rarely, if ever, does the actual translation. Publishing houses hire professional translators to do this work. Many grantwriters try to take a similar approach. They leave budget preparation to the accounting and bookkeeping wizards on the agency's staff, sometimes not even reading or reviewing what has been prepared. They're just thankful that the dreadful task of budget preparation is done. This is a mistake. Unlike authors, who do not need to be fluent in every language their works are translated into, grantwriters must be conversant with the language of numbers. At a minimum, they should be comfortable reviewing budgets, and the most versatile should be able to prepare them as well.

When a book is translated, say from English to Spanish, the vast majority of readers won't bother comparing the two versions to ensure that the translation is absolutely accurate. Yet grantmakers do compare the two versions that are submitted in the proposal package, namely the narrative story and the budget story. Funders expect both versions to be consistent. It's the grantwriter's job to make sure that these two versions are identical. The only way to do this is either to actively participate in preparing the budget or to thoroughly review the budget once someone else has prepared it.

This means you'll have to overcome numberphobia if you are afflicted. Take a workshop on understanding and preparing budgets for nonprofit agencies. Read a book on the subject. Reach out to professional colleagues who are willing to mentor you in developing a basic understanding of what a budget is. And by all means, keep reading this chapter.

WHAT THE BUDGET IS

The numbers story of a grant proposal begins with the budget. If grant funding is sought to support a specific program or project (remember that programs have an indefinite duration, whereas projects are short term), then a budget for that particular program or project needs to be prepared and attached to the proposal. Because agencies are likely to operate multiple programs, the budget for a specific program or project represents just a portion of an agency's overall annual budget. Therefore, the agency's annual budget is also attached along with the program budget. When seeking general operating support, however, there's only an annual budget to attach. (I discuss attachments and packing the proposal in greater detail in Chapter Ten.)

So what is a budget? It is a best estimate of how much the program will cost and how your agency plans to fund this cost. Budgets are divided into two sections: expected revenues and estimated expenses. Separate line items are listed for each source of projected revenue and each type of projected expense. Similar expenses are grouped together. For example, pens, pencils, paper, envelopes, erasers, rulers, and the like can all be bundled together under the category of office supplies. What the expense side of a budget really does is put a price tag on how the agency plans to respond to the story's antagonist (the problem or need) and deliver certain services to its clients. To put it another way, expenses put a price tag on methods.

A budget's length, detail, and complexity are directly related to the underlying narrative story. Large, complex programs necessitate large, complex budgets, whereas small programs require smaller, simpler budgets. Accordingly, the budget for a project costing an estimated $15,000 probably could be summarized on one page, whereas the budget for a $20 million program could run several pages.

Table 8.1 shows a sample budget for a small program.

Table 8.1
Sample Small Program Budget

	TOTAL CASH
Expected revenues	
Foundation grants	$10,000
Corporate grants	3,000
Total expected revenues	$13,000
Expected expenses	
Workshop trainer	$2,000
Program development	5,000
Administrative support	2,700
Photocopying	1,200
Postage and telephone	500
Site rental	800
Refreshments	400
Audiovisual equipment rental	400
Total expected expenses	$13,000

Budgets are forecasts, so funders don't expect applicant agencies to know all the specific costs or precisely where all the funds to cover those expenses will come from, especially if the request is for a brand-new program. However, funders do expect that an agency will make its best effort to determine what the income and expenses are most likely to be.

When working with budgets, it is also important to remember that they are not carved in stone, never to be changed. Budgets are fluid and flexible documents, forecasts that can be adjusted. During the course of the time period covered by a budget (typically your agency's fiscal year), the numbers can—and should—be updated and revised to accurately reflect your agency's story as it evolves.

Because grant proposals are submitted throughout the entire year, make certain that both the narrative story and the budget translation are updated as needed. Several things can happen to your nonprofit agency and its programs during the course of a year. As the months pass, perhaps more revenue is generated than originally anticipated and budgeted—and what a nice surprise that is! Sometimes expenses can come in lower than initially expected. In either of these circumstances, there's a surplus, and your agency has some important decisions to make. It can decide to expand the program, such as by increasing the number of clients served or by providing additional services to existing clients. Alternatively, your agency may conclude that it should hold on to the surplus and apply it to the following year's program expenses. Under either scenario, the initial budget will need to be adjusted to reflect the new financial reality.

Of course, the opposite financial story can occur: either less money comes in or expenses exceed original projections. If either of these situations arise, your nonprofit agency will need to undertake some cost-cutting measures. This could mean reducing program services and possibly serving fewer people. And once again, a new, revised budget must be prepared.

If you have proposals pending with potential funders, you should submit a revised budget whenever significant changes have been made. This keeps the funder fully informed and also provides you with another opportunity to contact and develop a relationship with the funder.

HOW TO BUDGET FOR CONTINUING PROGRAMS

Preparing a budget for a program that is continuing is easier than creating one for a brand-new one. With an ongoing program, you can refer to the program's prior fiscal history by reviewing the prior year's revenues and expenses. With this information as a base, you can prepare a new budget for the following year.

First, let's focus on the income portion of the budget. Looking at a program's previous funding history, you should be able to make some reasonable estimates about whether such funding will continue and (ideally) increase or whether there are circumstances that may cause financial support to decrease. Consider whether new funding sources have been identified and whether new strategies will be implemented. For example, will your agency be launching a major-donor campaign in the forthcoming year? Will it be increasing the size of its development staff? Or has a government funding program been eliminated? With answers to these types of questions, you can prepare a fairly accurate revenue section of your budget.

A similar analysis takes place when reviewing prior expenses and preparing the expense section of the budget. In determining future costs, take into account two factors. First, factor in inflation. Program costs always seem to go up. Rent skyrockets, insurance and utility rates rise, salaries are adjusted for inflation, and the cost of supplies steadily creeps up. New budgets for continuing programs must reflect these adjustments. Second, consider whether the program objectives and methods will change in the new grant period. If your agency plans to expand the delivery of its program services and reach more clients or if it seeks to enhance the program (even without reaching additional clients), expenses are likely to increase. And the program's new budget should reflect these changes.

HOW TO BUDGET FOR NEW PROGRAMS

When developing a budget for a new program or project, you do not have the advantage of looking to the past in order to forecast the future. What do you do? Throw your hands up in despair? Because this will not get you where you want to go, I recommend that you do something much more productive in building a budget for a new endeavor.

First, if possible, contact colleagues at other nonprofit organizations that have been running similar programs for a few years. Ask these folks what the most significant budgeting decisions were that they had to make in the program's earlier years. Invite them to share with you the budgeting lessons they learned along the way. During my years in the nonprofit field, I have found my colleagues at other institutions to be most generous with their time and knowledge. Don't be afraid to build collegial relationships and make fact-finding calls when necessary.

Second, do your own research, especially for the expense side of the equation. It will take a little time and effort to find out what most budget items will cost—from major pieces of equipment to office supplies to staff and contract personnel. Contact product vendors and compare prices. Price shopping online has made this task easier, and I have found that when merchants think they may have an upcoming sale, they are usually more than happy to provide price quotes.

Third, be conservative when budgeting for a brand-new program. On the income side, this means not overestimating projected revenues; on the expense side, it means not underestimating program costs. Demonstrating such fiscal prudence in a budget sends a strong positive message to potential funders. It says that your nonprofit agency makes sound judgments, is financially responsible, and is likely to deliver on the promises stated in the proposal. These are qualities that well-run agencies possess—and they're the ones that usually get the money!

A NOTE ABOUT BUDGET NOTES

There's one thing budget stories have that most proposal narrative stories do not (and this may be of some comfort to those who are numberphobic): notes in which words are used to explain the numerical tale more fully. In Chapter Five, I stated that footnotes are almost never used in the narrative text of a grant proposal. The budget section is an exception to this "rule." Budget notes can and often should be used, for they help explain and clarify the information contained in the numbers story.

When should you include budget notes? Two situations come to mind. A rule of thumb that I recommend is to consider including a note whenever an expense item represents 5 percent or more of the total estimated costs for the program. For example, assume a program budget of $100,000. If any individual line item equals or exceeds $5,000, I think about including a budget note to explain or justify that expense item. Second, you'll want to include a budget note whenever a particular line item might be unclear to the reader or might require additional narrative detail. For example, a line item labeled "miscellaneous" practically begs for a note to explain what is included under this category. (Examples of budget notes are included in the sample budget later in this chapter.)

EXPECTED REVENUES: MORE DETAIL

Whether writing the budget story for a continuing program or for one that is brand new, be certain to include all sources of projected revenues. For example, expected revenues may include one or more of the following:

- *Fee-for-service income.* This is the money paid by clients for the services provided by your nonprofit agency.

- *Unrelated business income.* These are moneys earned from activities operated by the nonprofit agency that are totally unrelated to the core work and mission of the agency. For example, a contemporary theater group operated a highly successful and very profitable business of recording dramatic audio tours used by various tourist sites nationwide. Although the income earned from such profit-making endeavors is taxed at corporate rates, it does help increase overall agency revenues.

- *Grants.* Because grants are awarded by foundations, corporations, and government agencies, you may want to separate anticipated grant revenues by the type of grantmaking entity.

- *Income from special fundraising events.* When projecting revenues from fundraising events, be sure that your calculation is based on net, not gross, income. In other words, make certain that you deduct the costs associated with holding the fundraising event when determining how much money you hope to reap from the event.

- *Contributions.* Individuals represent the largest source of philanthropic giving, accounting for approximately 85 percent of all charitable contributions annually. Your agency may receive donations from individuals through various channels, such as appeal letters, major gifts, and special gifts. Some donations may be earmarked for a particular program rather than being unrestricted. For example, a special mail appeal may be sent to individual donors for support of a specific program. Individual contributions raised or earmarked for a particular program would then be listed as a separate line item in the revenue portion of the budget.

- *Endowment income.* In some circumstances, an endowment fund may have been established to help cover the costs of a particular agency program. Interest income earned on the endowed funds would also be reported as a separate line item.

EXPECTED EXPENSES: MORE DETAIL

Whereas potential revenue sources are relatively few in number, possible expense items can be numerous and quite varied, depending on the type, scope, and size of the program. Some items (such as the cost for musical instruments) may be program specific. Other costs are more universal. The costs most likely to show up on almost every program budget are the following:

• *Salaries.* Personnel costs are frequently the major expense item in any program budget, and often these are underestimated. When a nonprofit agency develops a new program, special attention should be paid to determining what personnel are necessary to do the job and how many hours, days, weeks, or months will be required to get each individual task done.

It is not unusual for staff at nonprofit agencies to hope for unpaid volunteer assistance for certain activities. But agencies should consider what will happen if an inadequate number of volunteers sign up or if the volume of work exceeds the number of volunteer workers. Should more paid staff be hired? And if so, what are the budget ramifications?

It is a good practice to use a separate line item for each full- or part-time staff member rather than to lump all personnel costs together. Doing so makes it clear to the funder how salary costs will be allocated among different staff members.

• *Employee benefits.* If you aren't incorporating employee benefits (such as employer-paid taxes, worker's compensation, medical and dental insurance coverage, and retirement plans) into your salary calculations, then you aren't including all personnel costs in your program budget. Given that fringe benefits may equal as much as 25 percent or more of salaries, failing to include this item is a huge budgeting error. It is simply too big a number to omit. And it is probably better practice to list benefits as a separate line item, rather than to include benefits with the salary line item, in all but the simplest, smallest program budgets.

• *Contract personnel.* In today's nonprofit environment, additional professional expertise or temporary staff assistance is often acquired by retaining independent contractors rather than by hiring additional staff. If your agency plans to retain contract personnel, then the cost of doing so should be reflected in the budget. Furthermore, a budget note may be needed in order to describe the type of work being done by any independent contractor. A budget note may also be necessary if more than one independent contractor will be retained for the project.

- *Rent*. Rent is often another large expense item in an agency's overall annual budget. In certain circumstances, a portion of an agency's rental costs may also be included in a program budget. (How to do this will be discussed a little further along in this chapter.)

- *Equipment*. When developing a new program or improving an existing one, don't forget to include any special equipment needs in the budget. These may include the purchase of computers, medical testing devices, a vehicle, or any item that will be used specifically and exclusively for the program at hand. The consequences of not allocating these items in the budget can be serious. It may mean that the program does without or that funding must come out of the agency's general budget, thereby reducing funds earmarked for some other agency purpose.

- *Other expense items*. As previously noted, program costs can be many and varied, depending on the unique features of each program. Among the other nonpersonnel expenses your program may have are costs for telephones, photocopying, printing, insurance, supplies, travel, membership dues, and conferences. Be certain to carefully consider all of these smaller expenses your agency may incur in running its program. Individually, these costs may seem minor, but added together, they can represent a significant portion of a program budget.

OTHER COSTS THAT CAN BE ALLOCATED IN A PROGRAM BUDGET

Executive directors and other nonprofit professionals frequently lament that there simply aren't enough grantmakers willing to fund general operating expenses. Admittedly, it is challenging to secure unrestricted funding, and grant-seekers must be smart when approaching funders for general support. The good news is that certain expenses that might otherwise be considered as agency overhead or general operating costs can be included in a program budget. Shifting overhead costs from the overall agency budget to a program budget provides some financial relief to the agency.

Take an executive director's salary, for instance. It's an administrative expense, right? Not always. That portion of an executive director's time spent supervising a specific program can legitimately be allocated to the program budget. As a general guideline, I suggest that the allocated time be "significant"; otherwise, doing the calculation is more trouble than it's worth. It seems to me that "significant" means at least 10 percent or more of the executive director's time.

For example, an agency that treats injured wild animals and then releases healthy animals back to the wild plans to launch an educational program geared toward school-age children in grades 4 through 8. The agency develops a budget, which includes costs for hiring a full-time education coordinator, developing curriculum materials, and promoting the program to local schools and teachers.

The executive director estimates that he will spend one day each week (that is, 20 percent of his time) supervising the education coordinator and doing other administrative work related to the program. It is legitimate for a portion of the executive director's salary, in this case 20 percent, to be included in the program budget, for he will spend 20 percent of his time on the program. If the executive director's annual salary is $90,000, then it is appropriate to include $18,000 in the budget. Furthermore, an amount equal to 20 percent of costs for the executive director's employee benefits may also be allocated to the education program budget.

As illustrated in the preceding example, it is possible for a portion of an executive director's salary to be allocated to a program budget. Other administrative costs, such as dedicated clerical support for the program and office rent, may be properly allocated as well. The following are key questions to consider:

- Is significant administrative staff time going to be spent on program-specific activities?

- Is a portion of the nonprofit's office or other facility space going to be dedicated exclusively to serving the interests of the program? If so, is the square footage (or other acceptable measurement of the amount of space) that will be dedicated to the program reasonably easy to calculate?

As noted earlier with the example of the executive director's salary, I usually rely on the "10 percent rule" to guide me in deciding when to allocate these types of costs. If it is estimated that a staff member will spend at least 10 percent of his or her time working with the program, then I include it in the program budget. The same is true for rental costs. If a specific program occupies 10 percent or more of a nonprofit's facility, then I include the allocation. The rationale is that if an agency stopped operating the program, it could reduce its space requirements and thereby reduce its rental costs.

TAKE ONLY ONE BITE OF THE APPLE

Now one caveat: you can't take two bites out of the same budget apple. Two methods can be used in allocating what would otherwise be overhead costs to a program. You must choose only one of them. The first is what I have already described: a calculation based on estimates of actual costs (such as the percentage of the executive director's time devoted to a particular program). This method is easiest to use when costs and budgets are relatively small and when you can easily attribute specific costs to a program.

The second method is to use a single percentage for all overhead costs. This method is often selected when programs and their accompanying budgets are large and complex and when it is difficult, if not impossible, to specifically attribute a cost to a program. For example, is it possible to allocate a percentage of audit costs to each agency program? What about a receptionist's salary? Or insurance premiums? Certain expenses are darn near impossible to apportion. To cover these types of expenses, you may decide to include an "overhead" line item and assign a percentage.

What percentage is acceptable to use? Unfortunately, there is no simple answer. With some government grants, the granting agency makes it easy by printing the overhead percentage on the application form itself, and I've seen figures ranging from 7 to 17 percent. In the absence of direction from the potential grantmaker, the guiding principles I use are common sense, fairness, and prudence. I ask what's reasonable given all the circumstances, including the complexity of the program, the difficulties encountered in making actual estimates, and the sensibilities of the potential grantmaker. I've seen calculations range from a low of 5 percent to a high of 30 percent. I've also encountered grantmakers that will not fund the overhead portion of a budget and some that reject budgets entirely if they include overhead. As I've pointed out several times previously, it pays to know the funder's preference and to follow it.

INCLUDING IN-KIND CONTRIBUTIONS

Another consideration in budget preparation involves in-kind contributions. *In-kind contributions* are goods and services—something other than money— donated to an agency. For many nonprofit agencies, in-kind contributions represent a significant and valuable portion of their budgets. Accordingly, to overlook in-kind contributions when preparing a program or project budget would be a huge oversight. If these are not included, the budget does not accurately reflect the true program costs. Without these in-kind contributions, the agency would have to pay for these goods and services. It is beneficial for a nonprofit agency to secure in-kind contributions whenever possible. First, doing so means that your agency will have more cash to spend on other items in its budget. Second, like donated dollars, in-kind contributions demonstrate that there is strong community support for the agency.

Create an In-Kind column next to the Cash column in your budgets. Place all in-kind contributions, by line item, in this column. As an example, if your agency anticipates spending $5,000 for printing expenses and expects to receive an additional $2,500 in donated printing, the relevant portion of your budget would look like this:

Expenses	Cash	In-Kind	Total
Printing	$5,000	$2,500	$7,500

A balanced budget is one in which anticipated revenues equal anticipated expenses. Both key budget numbers—total revenues and total expenses—are the same. When your agency anticipates receiving in-kind contributions, the total amount of such donations must be included in both the revenue and expense portions of your budget. (Revenues are typically listed first, followed by expenses.) Carefully examine the sample large program budget shown in Table 8.2 to see how this is done. (The budget notes are shown at the bottom of the budget page in this example; alternatively, however, they may be attached on a separate piece of paper.)

CASH FLOW ANALYSIS

Preparing a cash flow analysis for your agency's program or project is critical, yet it is frequently overlooked in the scramble to design and launch a new initiative. Yet not preparing one can doom even the most well planned and fully funded program. Why? To understand the answer to that question, one must first understand the function of a cash flow analysis. The purpose of a cash flow analysis is to illustrate the ebb and flow of money coming into and going out of your nonprofit agency for a particular program. A cash flow analysis projects whether or not your agency will have sufficient funds on hand to pay program-related

Table 8.2
Sample Large Program Budget

	Cash	In-Kind	Total
Expected revenues			
Foundation grants	$100,000	$—	$100,000
Corporate grants	55,000	—	55,000
Government grants	25,000	—	25,000
Contributions from individuals[1]	40,000	—	40,000
Income from special events (net) [2]	30,000	—	30,000
Fee-for-service income	20,000	—	20,000
In-kind contributions	—	12,500	12,500
Total expected revenues	$270,000	$12,500	$282,500
Personnel expenses			
Program director[3]	$62,500	$—	$62,500
Program assistant	40,000	—	40,000
Administrative assistant	28,000	—	28,000
Executive director[4]	18,000	—	18,000
Consultant[5]	15,000	—	15,000
Facilitator[6]	—	7,500	7,500
Employee benefits[7]	37,125	—	37,125
Total personnel expenses	$200,625	$7,500	$208,125
Nonpersonnel expenses			
Office rent[8]	$36,000	$—	$36,000
Insurance	3,500	—	3,500
Office equipment[9]	10,000	2,000	12,000
Printing[10]	6,000	3,000	9,000
Photocopying	2,500	—	2,500
Postage	2,500	—	2,500
Telephone	2,750	—	2,750
Office supplies	1,000	—	1,000

(Continued on page 126)

Table 8.2 (*Continued*)

Travel	1,200	—	1,200
Professional development	1,500	—	1,500
Membership dues	1,000	—	1,000
Contingency	1,425	—	1,425
Total nonpersonnel expenses	$69,375	$5,000	$74,375
Total expected expenses	$270,000	$12,500	$282,500

[1] Our board of directors has pledged $15,000 for this program.

[2] Our agency plans to hold a special fundraising event this fall and anticipates net income of $30,000.

[3] The program director's salary is based on a countywide salary survey, which shows that full-time comparable positions are paid $55,000 to $67,000.

[4] The executive director expects to spend 20 percent of her time supervising this program during its first year ($90,000 × .20 = $18,000).

[5] A consultant is needed to develop the training and curriculum materials.

[6] A professional facilitator has agreed to provide pro bono services valued at $7,500.

[7] Employee benefits (employer-paid taxes, health and dental insurance, and long-term disability insurance) are calculated at 25 percent of salaries.

[8] Office rent is calculated at 30 percent of our agency's annual rent of $120,000.

[9] Program-specific office equipment needs include two computers, a printer, a fax machine, a digital camera, two workstations, two telephones, and software. One computer and software will be donated by a local merchant.

[10] One-third of the program's estimated printing costs will be donated by a local printer.

expenses as they come due. Therefore, it is customary for a cash flow analysis to be done on a month-by-month basis.

If a cash flow analysis reveals that your agency will have less money on hand in any given month than it will need to pay its bills, then the agency must plan for this reality and make whatever fiscal adjustments are necessary. Not having enough available cash is fairly common at the early stages of a program. To get the program up and running, a nonprofit agency often incurs a lot of up-front costs, yet funding—even committed grant funding—may not arrive until later. This means that an agency may have to temporarily dip into its general operating funds in order to pay these program start-up expenses. It's better to know this information sooner rather than later. A cash flow analysis is thus an excellent planning tool.

Note that a cash flow analysis is not usually included with the proposal submission. This is an internal document for you to use in program planning.

Table 8.3 shows what a cash flow analysis looks like. In this example, the program does not realize a positive cash flow until the fourth month of operation. Funds must therefore be available from other sources (most likely from the agency's general operating fund) to pay program costs during its early months of operation.

FINANCIAL STATEMENTS

A budget translates the proposal's narrative story into numbers, forecasting projected income and expenses. In contrast, a current financial statement is an accounting of your agency's most recent fiscal history. Think of financial statements as historical documents. They inform the reader of what actually happened with the agency's money—where it came from (revenue) and how it was spent (expenses)—and report the total amount of agency assets at the beginning of the fiscal year and their value at the end of that period. A thorough review of a nonprofit agency's recent financial statements reveals trends and can indicate whether an agency is fiscally sound or swimming in a sea of red ink. Depending on what they report, financial statements will either substantiate or detract from your written narrative story.

For instance, there's a problem if a proposal narrative states that a nonprofit agency is well run, financially stable, and growing, yet the financial statements report a deficit (that is, the agency spent more money than it collected during the relevant fiscal period). This discrepancy can cause the funder to question the agency's credibility. How well is an agency being managed if it is operating in the red? How will it be possible for the agency to grow and to launch new programs if it must first cover old debts? Given the agency's fiscal reality, it would be appropriate for the proposal story to address the agency's financial issues head-on by answering the following questions: Does the agency have a sound fiscal plan to reduce its debt? Does management have the experience and financial knowledge to lead the agency going forward? Does the board of directors have a financial committee?

Grantmakers almost always request that an agency's most recent financial statements be attached with the grant proposal narrative, so there's no hiding or escaping from your agency's financial history. It is there for the grantmaking world to see. And although your agency cannot rewrite its history, it has an opportunity—and an obligation—to tell its current story, both in words and numbers, as accurately as possible.

Table 8.3
Sample Cash Flow Analysis

	January	February	March	April	May	June
Revenues						
Foundation grants	$—	$—	$10,000	$20,000	$20,000	$15,000
Corporate grants	—	5,000	—	25,000	10,000	—
Government grants	—	—	—	—	—	25,000
Contributions from individuals	—	—	—	—	—	—
Income from special events (net)	—	—	—	—	30,000	—
Fee-for-service income	—	—	2,000	2,000	2,000	2,000
Total revenues	$—	$5,000	$12,000	$47,000	$62,000	$42,000
Expenses						
Salaries and benefits	$15,000	$15,000	$15,000	$15,000	$15,000	$15,000
Consultant	—	5,000	5,000	5,000	—	—
Office rent	10,000	10,000	10,000	10,000	10,000	10,000

Insurance	300	300	300	300	300	300
Printing	—	—	6,000	—	—	—
Photocopying	—	500	500	500	500	500
Postage	100	100	2,000	100	100	100
Telephone	225	225	225	225	225	225
Office supplies	250	250	100	100	50	50
Travel	1,000	—	—	—	—	—
Professional development	—	—	1,000	—	—	—
Membership dues	500	—	—	—	—	—
Total expenses	$27,375	$31,375	$40,125	$31,225	$26,175	$26,175
Net cash flow	$(27,375)	$(26,375)	$(28,125)	$15,775	$35,825	$15,825

SUMMARY

Stories may be written in one language and then translated into another. When seeking grants, we have narrative proposals and budgets. Budgets translate our story into the language of numbers. You'll need to be conversant with this language if you are to be successful in your grantseeking. Having an understanding of the following key points should help:

- A budget is a forecast of expected revenues and expenses.

- An agency has an overall annual budget detailing all of its anticipated revenues and expenses. It should also have a separate budget for each program for which it plans to seek grant funding.

- Budget notes explain or clarify individual line items when how the number was derived isn't clear.

- Appropriate administrative costs can be incorporated into a program budget. There are two methods for doing so: an estimate of actual costs or a flat percentage. Choose one or the other.

- In-kind contributions should be included in your program budgets.

- A cash flow analysis projects the timing of when expenses must be paid and income can be expected.

- Financial statements reveal an agency's prior financial history.

The Summary, Titles, and Headings

Preparing Your Marketing Copy

Imagine you're about to go on a well-deserved weeklong sojourn to a tropical beach. There you are at the airport, when suddenly you remember that you forgot to pack something to read for those seven blissful days lying in a lounge chair. You scurry over to the airport bookstore, which is stacked floor to ceiling with the latest paperbacks. The only trouble is that you've been working so hard that you have no idea which of the books is a literary masterpiece and which is trash. How do you decide among the thousand or more titles?

If you're like most of us, you'll first narrow the selection down to a particular topic or genre, or perhaps look for a new release by a favorite author. Then you're likely to scan the titles. A few sound interesting, perhaps even intriguing. You pick a book off the shelf and turn it over to read the jacket. There, with an economy of words, the book jacket blurb distills the essence of the plot. If it is engaging, so compelling that you can't put the book down, you'll make a purchase. If you do, the teaser copy on the book jacket has done what it is supposed to do: it convinced you to buy the book. Once you've made the investment, you're likely at least to crack the book open.

WHY THE SUMMARY IS LIKE A BOOK JACKET

There are several similarities between the bookstore scenario and what happens inside foundation, corporate, and government offices all across the country when proposals are being reviewed. Think of grant proposals as the array of available books. In many ways, a program officer or other proposal reviewer is a lot like we are when we visit a bookstore. For practical reasons, we often can buy only one, two, or maybe a handful of books at any one time. Likewise, the great majority of potential grantmakers can fund just a fraction of the many proposals they receive.

You'll recall that, on average, the ratio of proposals submitted to those funded is about ten or twelve to one. And the number of submissions to any given funder can be staggering. It is not uncommon for a grantmaker to receive hundreds, if not thousands, of proposals in a giving cycle. Facing this kind of volume, do program officers really read all these submissions from cover to cover? Not always. That's just impractical. The sheer quantity of reading material, when layered upon telephone calls, meetings, and site visits, is too great. So what do many program officers do? How do they get some control over the avalanche of proposals?

Just as you probably have certain types or genres of books that you prefer to read, program officers have initial screening criteria for choosing those proposals they are more likely to read thoroughly. Their initial screening criteria are based on the funding priorities of the foundation. Program officers read just enough of a submitted proposal to determine whether it fits within their foundation's giving priorities. The first sentence or two of a proposal may tell them all they need to know and whether or not they should continue reading.

For example, suppose the Schwalbe Family Foundation has decided to exclusively fund nonprofit agencies working in the area of adult literacy in Milwaukee, Wisconsin, and this criterion is stated clearly in the foundation's guidelines. If the foundation receives a proposal that begins "The Save the Centipede Society requests a $10,000 grant to support our larva hatchling program in Manhattan," the program officer wouldn't need to read another word. This proposal simply does not fit within the foundation's established giving criteria. The program officer can place this one in the rejection pile and pick up the next submission. With most grantmakers, this is how the process works. The reviewer creates two piles. In one pile go all the submissions that obviously do not fit within the grantmaker's prescribed areas of funding. The second pile contains those that at least at first glance appear to fit within the grantmaker's funding criteria.

A grantmaker's initial screening process is therefore similar to the mental process each of us uses while scanning the bookstore shelves: "Romance? No. Western? No. Science fiction? Eureka!" Once we find the right section of the bookstore, we begin to scan the shelves and may come across an intriguing title: "Aha! *Revenge of the Three-Toed Space Aliens.*" If we do, we may actually take the book off the shelf and read the book jacket.

The proposal summary—the part of the proposal that the reader sees first—is similar to the copy on a book jacket. Just as the book jacket summarizes the contents of the book, the proposal summary encapsulates the proposal's narrative in a limited amount of space, perhaps only a paragraph or two. The summary must not only demonstrate that the proposal fits within the funder's guidelines but also immediately engage the reader. The function of the summary, like that of a book jacket, is to "sell" the narrative—to motivate the reader to make a further investment of time, open the proposal, turn to the next page.

WRITE THE SUMMARY AFTER THE PROPOSAL

As is true with the copy on a book jacket, the summary is written last, after you've finished the rest of the proposal narrative. I challenge anyone to write her proposal summary before she has written the full proposal itself. It's impossible. A grantwriter must draft all the other sections of the narrative first, then prepare the summary. An author finishes a book before she or the publisher crafts the book jacket text. That copy is drawn from and based on what actually happens in the pages between the two covers. The same is true with a grant proposal.

When starting to draft a proposal, we may think we have all the information we'll need to write a complete narrative. But inevitably, as we begin writing, we think of new questions that require answers from program staff, the executive director, or our agency's finance department. Occasionally, new or additional information surfaces that needs to be incorporated. Preparing a grant proposal is as fluid and creative a process as writing a book or short story. It's best to go with the flow. Therefore, save yourself some time and agony: write the summary last.

THE SUMMARY'S SIGNIFICANCE

If you consider the summary the "book jacket" of your proposal, you'll realize that this is not some throwaway section that can be cranked out at the last minute or when you're tired and weary. The summary is crucial. Significant funding decisions are frequently made on the basis of the summary alone. Accordingly, it deserves your undivided, careful attention. When you are writing the summary, word choice is important. Use dynamic, energetic words. Use the present or future tense. Avoid the passive voice. Be bold. Be brief.

In most cases, we don't have a choice when it comes to being brief with the summary. Many grantmakers will prescribe that the summary must be limited to a certain number of words. It is common to see limits in the 100- to 250-word range. For online submissions and on printed grant application forms, the space restrictions may be even more severe. We must convey the essence of our request as succinctly as possible.

WHAT THE SUMMARY MEANS TO GRANTMAKERS: AN INSIDER'S VIEW

I've always worked on the grantseeking side of the table, not the grantmaking side. Over the years, however, I have attended dozens of funder panels and have comoderated more than a dozen "reality grantmaking" sessions where real funders review real proposals in real time and award the best with a $1,000 minigrant. I have friends and professional colleagues who serve as program officers, foundation trustees, and members of employee contribution committees. These individuals have candidly shared with me their thoughts and observations about the inner workings of a funder's office. One of the most helpful tidbits I've picked up concerns the proposal summary. Let me explain.

As you may know, your agency's proposal is not likely to be reviewed by the ultimate decision makers (that is, the board of trustees) at many foundations. When a foundation, usually one that is medium size or larger, has a professional staff, the initial screening of proposals falls squarely on the program officer's shoulders.

By screening proposals, program officers are sifting out those that clearly don't fit within their funding guidelines. Generally, proposals that do fit receive a thorough, careful review. In some circumstances, program officers are delegated some funding authority and can award small grants (often in the range of $5,000 or less) without first seeking board approval (or having the board review the request).

In those situations when the ultimate funding decision is made by a foundation's board of trustees, it is customary for the program officer to prepare a list of funding recommendations based on his or her review and analysis of all submissions in that particular funding cycle. It is not atypical for the program officer's funding recommendations to exceed the total dollars available for distribution. It's the job of the trustees to make the final decisions. What the program officer has done is narrow the choices. To assist the trustees in making their decision, program officers are often required to prepare a briefing paper, generally only one page long, that summarizes each proposal being recommended for funding.

Here's the secret I learned: program officers sometimes lift the summary from the original proposal verbatim and copy it onto their briefing paper. When does this happen? When the program officer can't write the summary of your request any better than you already have. In these cases, our words are actually read by the foundation trustees. They aren't reading a summary of a summary, somebody else's words and phrases. They're reading our own creative copy.

This suggests that there are several reasons why you should invest serious time in crafting the "book jacket" portion of each proposal. First, your agency wants to promote its proposal to the potential funder, and you want your story to receive a careful, critical review. Second, you may be helping out an overwhelmed program officer who's working on a tight deadline by enabling that person simply to use your summary when preparing the required briefing materials that are presented to the trustees. Finally, if your summary is so well written that the program officer uses it verbatim in a presentation to the board of trustees, the trustees (though you will probably never know it) will read your exact words, the ones so carefully chosen to describe your agency's request for funding. Now that's powerful.

I think examples are powerful too, for showing is more effective than telling. I've told you my tips for writing stronger summaries. Now take a look at Examples 9.1 and 9.2, which showcase this advice.

PERSUASIVE TITLES AND HEADINGS: A FEW CAREFULLY CHOSEN WORDS

I recommend naming your agency's programs and projects and using section headings in proposals. When thoughtfully crafted, program titles and section headings serve as additional "marketing copy" for your request and help "sell" your proposal to the potential grantmaker.

Example 9.1
Summary for a Blood Bank

Blood Centers of the Pacific (BCP) is a nonprofit community-based organization dedicated to providing a safe, adequate, and affordable supply of blood and blood components to patients throughout Northern California. BCP receives approximately 50% of all blood donations at on-site blood drives that are held almost daily throughout the region—and almost half of these blood drives are dependent on our donor mobile coaches. Currently, BCP has three self-contained donor coaches that serve a broad geographical area stretching from San Jose in the south to Redding in the north, and from San Francisco east to Vallejo.

However, BCP's donor mobile coaches are not new; in fact, one is seemingly traveling "on fumes" these days. Therefore, it is our goal to replace at least one donor coach and hopefully add an additional donor coach within the next year. Having three, and possibly four, dependable donor coaches will enable BCP to continue to provide Northern Californians with a safe, available, and affordable blood supply for years to come.

Example 9.2
Summary for Urban Shakespeare

Urban Shakespeare provides at-risk, disadvantaged young people (ages 13 to 18) with theater training and engages them in the study of Shakespeare. Our intensive 16-week program teaches teens valuable literacy skills as it builds their self-confidence and provides a means for constructive self-expression. Urban Shakespeare also strives to demystify Shakespeare's poetic language by making it relevant to participating teens and contemporary urban life.

This highly regarded program is offered free of charge to young people living in our region's most underserved urban areas, yet our program costs are actually $1,500 per participant. Therefore, we must seek critical financial underwriting from local grantmakers in order to continue to make this program possible. This is why Urban Shakespeare is submitting this proposal to the Horton Charitable Fund.

Program Titles

Why should your agency give its programs and projects a title? (Recall that programs are ongoing activities, whereas projects are of a shorter, limited duration.) A program title serves as a shorthand description of the program itself. If accurate, the title immediately tells the reader whether or not the program fits within the funder's giving priorities. For that reason, it's an important marketing and sales tool. Think of a title as similar to a billboard or an advertisement for your program.

Accordingly, your agency—just like new parents selecting a baby's name—should thoughtfully consider the name for any new program for which it will be seeking funding support. A program title should be accurate, descriptive, and as creative as possible.

Some serious thought went into the program titles in the following three examples. Each is a compelling advertisement for the program itself and for the accompanying narrative story:

- "Saber Es Poder" ("Knowledge Is Power"). This is the apt and creative name of an outreach program created by San Francisco–based Breast Cancer Action to educate Latina women about breast cancer prevention and detection.

- "Ridge, Kids and Stewards." This title effectively captures the essence of an environmental education program for school-age children that encourages them to become environmental stewards. The program is offered by the Bay Area Ridge Trail Council, which is working toward establishing a four-hundred-mile trail encircling the San Francisco Bay.

- "College Connect." This is a new name that unifies all programming at Mission Graduates. Mission Graduates offers after-school enrichment programs for elementary and middle school programs; leadership, outdoor, and career-preparedness programs for high school students; plus workshops on college financial aid, the college application process, and similar topics for parents. The overarching theme of Mission Graduates programming is to prepare low-income, primarily Latino, youth to attend four-year colleges.

Program names matter. A strong or evocative program title conveys significant information. Make sure each word counts.

Time to Write!

Does your agency have an unnamed or unremarkably named program? Give renaming possibilities some thought. Perhaps pull a small group of staff members together for a short brainstorming session. What new titles can you come up with?

Section Headings

Section headings in proposal narratives deserve as much consideration as what to call an agency's programs. They too can serve as marketing or advertising copy. In keeping with my storytelling metaphor, section headings in a proposal are like chapter titles in a book. However, section headings are not merely word dividers that break a text into different segments. Section headings serve multiple purposes.

First, they serve as signage, as helpful markers that lead a reader through a proposal's written narrative. Program officers tell me that such word markers are most useful when they are trying to locate a specific section in the proposal. For example, a heading that reads "Problem Statement" is a good indication that the reader will find information documenting the need and why it exists in subsequent paragraphs. Second, section headings help break up dense copy, making it easier and more inviting for the reader. For a funder, there are few things more daunting than having to face pages and pages of text all in the same typeface and font. Third, section headings can be used to present persuasive information.

For these reasons, I suggest using section headings in longer narrative stories, such as those that run three to five pages or more. In shorter narratives, headings are not absolutely necessary, though you may want to consider using one or two even in a brief letter to break up copy. Without going overboard on the graphics, it is okay to use bold or italics for headings.

In many contemporary textbooks and workshops on grantseeking, grantwriters are instructed to march through the customary components of a proposal: summary, introduction, problem or needs statement, goals and objectives section, methods section, evaluation section, and future funding section. Consequently, most grantwriters use these exact words for the section headings in their proposals. Although this approach will certainly suffice (and I've done it in the past myself), it really squanders an opportunity to use language that more effectively engages the reader and markets your request. Instead of doing the ordinary, do the extraordinary and think of section headings as billboards for your proposal story.

Let's use the problem statement as an example. It is perfectly adequate to use "Problem Statement" as a section heading. Yet that's all it is: adequate. See how much more is conveyed when instead of "Problem Statement," the following headings are used:

- No Place to Go: Why There's an Overwhelming Need for a Neighborhood Recreation Center
- Problem Solved: New After-School Program Will Reduce Juvenile Crime
- Need for a Shuttle Bus: Independence and Flexibility for Seniors

These are three fine examples of how a section heading can really work to the agency's benefit. Each of these has more punch than the term "Problem Statement" alone. Notice, though, that each of the sample headings incorporates the word "need" or "problem." You don't want to sacrifice clarity for creativity. Make certain your headings clearly indicate the section of the proposal they are describing.

Perhaps you're now wondering how the history and mission or methods section headings can be spiced up. Here are some examples:

- 35 Years of Sheltering the Homeless
- The Symphony's 20-Year History of Musical Excellence
- Marin Horizon School Integrates Montessori Methodology in Curriculum
- Recycling Pilot Project Tests New Methods

Unfortunately, some online submissions make it impossible for us to include section headings. Instead, we are asked to fill in boxes and write text that is pre-set to a uniform typeface and font. It is my opinion, and that of more than a few program officers, that such format rigidity restricts the ability of the applicant agency to show its personality in the proposal. When every proposal looks identical, does every agency look identical? Personally, I prefer those online applications that permit at least some latitude regarding formatting and style.

Time to Write!

I invite you to pull out an old proposal, one in which you didn't include section headings or one where you used our "old faithful" language. Rewrite your headings as billboard copy. See if you can't be more creative this time around.

SUMMARY

What goes on a book jacket has great significance. Captivating jacket copy encourages people to buy and read the book. Similarly, a strong proposal summary can motivate a program officer to read the entire proposal—a crucial step toward securing funding. Program titles and section headings are opportunities to deliver persuasive information. Here's a summary of this chapter's key points for providing punch to your summaries, titles, and headings:

- You should write the entire proposal first and then the summary. When it comes time to organize your proposal, the summary comes first.

- Your words have power and influence. In some circumstances, a well-composed summary may be lifted verbatim by a program officer when preparing briefing materials for foundation trustees.

- Program titles describe the essence of your program.

- Section headings serve as guideposts, marking the way in a proposal. They are also billboards that help market your request.

Packaging
Publishing Your Proposal Story

Ahhh ... You've finished writing your agency's compelling story.
The proposal narrative is complete. Is it time to put your feet
up and rest? Get your feet off that desk! There's still some work to
do. A grant proposal is not finished just because the narrative is
written and you have an accompanying budget. As the saying goes,
"The devil's in the details." This is certainly true when it comes to
the next step in the grantseeking process, which is getting the proposal ready for submission to a potential funder.

Why can't you submit the story and be done with it? Imagine that you are judg-
ing a writing contest. From the more than one thousand entries you've received
by the deadline, you must pick thirty finalists, write a report on each of those top
entries, and be prepared to discuss each one at a meeting of all contest judges
in just four weeks. Let's face it: you'd be in a time crunch. When reviewing all
one thousand entries, you aren't going to be as patient with or as interested in
those that are visually difficult to read or disorganized, or that just don't follow
the contest guidelines. There are simply too many other worthy entries to bother
with those frustrating ones. Not surprisingly, program officers respond to the
mountains of submitted proposals in much the same way.

NO BOILERPLATE PROPOSALS

Executive directors, development directors, and other nonprofit professionals often ask me, "Can't we just create a boilerplate proposal that we can submit to all potential funders?" The answer is an emphatic no. To be successful in grantseeking, you can't draft a generic, one-size-fits-all grant proposal. You do not mass-produce a grant proposal and send the identical story to each potential funder.

It is true that once you have developed a proposal, much of the core text will be reusable in later submissions, perhaps as much as 80 to 90 percent of the narrative content. However, for every additional submission, expect to tailor and fine-tune your story. You want each proposal to "speak" directly to each grantmaker. You accomplish this by demonstrating alignment with the funder's giving priorities and by thoughtfully selecting words and phrases that will resonate with the funder.

As grantwriters, we are storytellers with a basic tale to tell: a story about our agency, the clients it serves, and the work it does. However, we don't need to, and we shouldn't, repeat the story exactly the same way with each funder. Instead, we have an opportunity to craft each proposal to the exact specifications of the grantmaker. We can be wonderfully creative and amend the story, to varying degrees, with each writing.

For example, suppose you work for a nonprofit agency that offers environmental education programs for school-age children in grades 1 through 5. When spinning your tale to those grantmakers that fund environmental programs, you should emphasize the environmental aspect of the program. In contrast, when approaching a funder that prioritizes elementary school education as a giving priority, you'd be wise to highlight this dimension of the program. In each respective proposal, you'd be writing about the same program, but your emphasis shifts appropriately.

Sometimes the smallest changes will have the greatest impact. When it comes to revising a proposal for a new funder, it is my experience that altering as little as 10 to 20 percent of the text can enhance your agency's chances of getting the grant manyfold. In the highly competitive grantseeking environment, this is a wise investment of your time.

APPLYING ONLINE

These days, more and more funders prefer electronic submissions. Although online submissions often are formatted with a series of questions that must be answered in a limited amount of space, I maintain that you can still use the storytelling approach I present in this book. Within the confines of these "boxed answers," you can still tell your story in a creative and engaging fashion. Online applications ask for information about your agency's history and mission, the need or problem being addressed, the intended outcomes, the program plan and description, your plan for evaluation and future funding—the same elements you must cover in a written proposal.

There are challenges, though, with the "packaging" of electronic submissions. One of my most frustrating experiences concerns those very rare (fortunately) online applications that will not let you save your document and return to it at a later date. My solution is to print the form, draft my responses, have my work reviewed by the client, make revisions, and then complete the form in one sitting and finish by hitting "submit."

Another frustration, albeit a more minor one, are those online applications that give you little or no control over style and formatting. Typeface and type size, margins, and the use of such features as bold, italics, and underlining may be preset by the software program. This eliminates your ability to emphasize certain words or numbers. I also believe that an agency's personality—whether formal or informal, structured or unstructured, serious or playful—is often revealed in a hard-copy proposal, especially by the choices made concerning style and formatting. This is also lost when all submissions look exactly the same.

One other major difference between an electronic submission and a paper one is that you don't have an opportunity to include a cover letter. On the one hand, because this is one less document you have to write, you might think this is a good thing. However, a cover letter gives you another opportunity to "sell" your request to a potential funder. And because cover letters are printed on your agency's letterhead, on which your agency's logo, tagline, and board of directors may appear, the funder learns a little bit more about your agency's personality.

Finally, I have encountered challenges electronically submitting attachments that are not already in electronic form. Most often, these have been an agency's 501(c)(3) letter and financial statements. Some funders understand the inherent difficulty in not having all required information in an electronic form and allow these materials to be submitted by posting them with the U.S. Postal Service. However, some do not seem to recognize the problem—or that scanning reams of paper isn't a realistic solution!

After reading this section, you may have concluded that I am not especially fond of electronic submissions. Actually, there are things I like about submitting online. I especially like the fact that usually the funder provides an organizational structure for submissions, generally through a series of questions that prompt responses. This is most helpful to beginning grantwriters and volunteers who are often intimidated by having to write from whole cloth. I also like that at least in theory we are saving paper by doing more work electronically, though I suspect that the majority of online proposals are printed out for hard-copy files at both ends of the process. However, I also believe that some nuances that can influence decision making are at risk of being lost through online applications.

ALL DRESSED UP AND SOMEPLACE TO GO: THE PACKAGING OF A PAPER SUBMISSION

Let's now consider issues that arise when filing a paper submission. A proposal's packaging, which includes everything from how the proposal actually looks physically to the attachments enclosed with it, is every bit as important as the narrative story.

In the publishing world, writing a good story is only part of a much bigger process. After a manuscript arrives at the publisher, there are all sorts of considerations that must be addressed before the story gets into print. Will a book debut in hardcover or go straight to paperback? What typeface should be used? Are illustrations needed? These are some of the questions that a publisher must answer. As grantwriters, we not only get to draft proposal stories but also function as publishers and have a long list of publishing decisions to make.

One of the first decisions concerns the overall look of the proposal. How does it appear on the page? Is it an attractive presentation? Neatness counts. Although substance prevails over style, make certain your proposal's first impression is a favorable one.

White Bond Paper

Type your proposal on plain, white bond paper. Resist the allure of colored paper stock. Sure, brilliant yellow is guaranteed to get your proposal noticed, but for the wrong reason. You want the reader to take notice of your proposal for the right reasons, most notably, that you've provided a well-written description of a worthwhile program. It is not necessary to copy the proposal on agency letterhead. Letterhead is expensive, and it detracts from the narrative story. Keep the look "classically elegant." Like a simple black dress, white bond paper is the answer to the perennial "what to wear?" question.

Ample Margins

Use a one-inch margin on all four sides of the paper. If a grantmaker gives a firm page limit, don't try to squeeze more words onto the page by narrowing the margins. The proposal will start looking crowded and not very inviting to read. Instead of trying to fit more copy on the page, try to eliminate some unnecessary words through careful editing. Great authors usually have excellent editors. If you're having difficulty staying within a prescribed page limit, have a colleague or friend with strong editing skills review the proposal and make suggestions for tightening your story and boiling it down to the key elements so that it fits.

Adequate Type Size

Choose either eleven- or twelve-point type. (Personally, the older I get, the more I appreciate a larger type size!) Occasionally a funder will specify that a minimum type size must be used. It's in your agency's best interest to honor this request, but when in doubt, apply the "eleven or twelve rule."

Single Spacing

Whether to double-space or not, that is the question. There's some latitude regarding this decision. Some grantmakers may specify a preference, and if so, always give them what they want. When there is no guidance, the decision is yours. As a general rule, I single-space my proposals. In an era when we are all concerned about paper waste, conservation, and recycling, it seems more prudent to single-space whenever possible. I make certain, though, to provide enough white space by using one-inch margins and double-spacing between paragraphs and sections. Adequate white space is important, for it gives the eye a visual "resting place" in long narratives.

Similar considerations apply when it comes to whether or not to use double-sided copies. Some grantmakers are very specific in their preference, and if so, follow the funder's instructions. When there are none, I suggest going with one-sided copies. My concern about double-sided copies is that sometimes print from one side bleeds through to the other side, interfering with readability. Also, readers may want to thumb through the proposal, scanning for the key points. This can only be done if the proposal is single sided. Ultimately, though, in the absence of instructions from the grantmaker, the decision is one of personal preference.

No Binders!

Now here's a hard-and-fast rule: don't use binders or folders. Grantmakers don't want proposals arriving in "fancy" packages. In fact, a pretty outer wrap can detract from the story itself and can give the impression that your agency has money to burn. There's also a practical reason why binders, folders, or even staples shouldn't be used: photocopying. Typically, the first thing that happens when a proposal reaches a funder's office is that the proposal is photocopied. But if the proposal is all bundled up like a baby in a blanket, someone must unwrap it before photocopying. That's a hassle. Remember, we don't want to annoy prospective grantmakers; we want to make their lives easier. In many instances, the funder will tell you precisely how to package the proposal. Follow these instructions to the letter, and you won't go wrong. One more piece of advice: rather than purchasing those binders, folders, and staples, invest in a box of giant paper clips. They do a great job of holding a proposal together.

At this point, the proposal narrative is all dressed up and ready to go. But it cannot go alone.

AN ESCORT FOR THE PROPOSAL: THE COVER LETTER

When submitting a full grant proposal, don't let it travel alone. A paper proposal needs to be accompanied by a cover letter. That's proper etiquette. Print your letter on agency letterhead. This ensures a professional look and also provides the reader with your agency's contact information (address, phone number, Web address).

If your letterhead doesn't contain the address and phone number you prefer the funder to use in contacting your agency, be sure to include this information in your cover letter. Mary Gregory, currently a vice president with Pacific Foundation Services, which manages several family foundations, notes that some agencies neglect this basic principle. She remarks on how frustrating—and damaging to a grantseeker's credibility—that can be. "Every once in a while," she says, "our office receives a proposal printed on plain paper, which is fine, but accompanied by a cover letter with no address or phone number (not fine!). We're not psychic. We need some way to respond. And aside from being aggravating, this kind of slip doesn't say good things about an agency's attention to detail."

Ideally, a cover letter is brief, generally one page consisting of three or four paragraphs. When drafting a cover letter, it's helpful to remember that it is just another vehicle for telling your agency's story.

What's said in a cover letter? Some information is a tad redundant, restating what's said in the proposal itself. However, a few new items are included in the typical cover letter. Here's the basic format I use:

- Acknowledge the prior support of the funder, if appropriate. Doing so both expresses the agency's gratitude and demonstrates to the funder that your agency maintains accurate records.

- Demonstrate in just a sentence or two that your agency's request fits within the funder's giving priorities. Tell the prospective grantmaker that your agency engages in work that the foundation or corporation values and feels is important.

- State the exact dollar amount of your agency's request. This amount should be within the typical dollar range of grants awarded by the funder. Again, this demonstrates that your agency has done its homework and has researched the appropriateness of this particular funder as a strong prospect. Requesting a grant outside the customary range of awards, especially if it is on the high side, indicates to the funder that your agency has not done its research or is naive in its expectations.

- Summarize the essence of your proposal story with a succinct statement of the community problem or unmet need and a brief description of your agency's proposed response to meet that need. Refer to the proposal summary and the proposal text in drafting this paragraph (or two). To avoid using redundant language, keep a thesaurus readily at hand. And if anyone comes up with a synonym for "support," please let me know!

- In the final paragraph, thank the funder for considering your request. You may want to officially extend an invitation to the program officer to make a site visit. However, it is not a requirement that you do so. If a program officer wants to visit your agency at any time during the review process, it is my experience that he or she will not hesitate to ask for one.

- Identify the primary contact person in the closing paragraph as well. The designated person should be someone who is easily accessible if the funder calls, which means that this may not always be the same person who signs the letter. For many medium-size and large agencies, the best contact person may not be the executive director because executive directors tend to keep busy, even frantic, schedules and are therefore not always able to return telephone calls quickly. So designating the development director, associate director, or grantwriter might be a more practical choice.

Finally, who signs the cover letter? Though a grantwriter or someone else on an agency's development staff may draft the cover letter, the senior executive at your agency should sign it. This could be your agency's executive director, a dean or head of school, an artistic director, or the board president.

Example 10.1 is a sample of an effective cover letter.

Example 10.1
Sample Cover Letter

Ms. Janice Promer
Program Officer
Give-away Foundation
2222 Foundation Parkway
San Francisco, CA 98765

Dear Ms. Promer:

   Two years ago, the Give-away Foundation generously gave Blood Centers of the Pacific (BCP) grant funding to purchase a new donor mobile coach, for which we are very grateful. That wonderful new donor coach has already traveled thousands of miles throughout the San Francisco Bay Area helping us collect much-needed blood for trauma victims and patients undergoing surgery. On behalf of all those individuals who received this donated blood, we once again thank the Give-away Foundation for its previous grant.

   Today we write to the Give-away Foundation to request new funding support. We seek a grant of $120,000 to purchase medical equipment

---

that will better enable BCP to collect and store donated blood and plasma. Specifically, we hope to purchase three new plasma collection machines, as well as one new replacement plasma freezer. Additionally, we need twenty tube sealers, which are relatively simple devices, yet they serve an important purpose by helping to ensure the safety of collected whole blood.

Plasma is a critical component of blood; it is the fluid that transports red and white cells and other blood components through the body. Plasma is often needed by patients suffering major trauma, bleeding disorders, and shock and burns, as well as by those undergoing many complex medical procedures, such as liver transplants. With an ever-increasing Bay Area population and advances in medical care that make procedures like liver transplants possible, there is a growing need for plasma. BCP strives to meet this need. This year BCP hopes to double the number of its collection centers able to collect plasma from three to six by purchasing three new plasma collection machines. And because plasma must be frozen within six hours of collection, BCP also hopes to replace an old, worn-out plasma freezer that is currently being used in our Fairfield center. We also need to replace twenty tube sealers, which are used to seal the bags of collected blood, thereby preventing contamination.

In an era of managed health care, BCP operates on a lean budget given the size of our operations and the critical nature of our work. This is why we must ask for financial support from the community to acquire important medical equipment. We hope that the Give-away Foundation will once again invest in our organization.

We appreciate your consideration of our grant request. Enclosed is a complete grant application form along with the requested attachments. If you need additional information or have any questions, please do not hesitate to contact either our development assistant, Howard Rosenberg, at 111-111-1111, or me at 111-111-1112.

Sincerely,

Nora Hirschler, MD
President and Chief Executive Officer

Time to Write!

So far, you've been resting in this chapter, but now it's time to write. First, identify a grantmaker already known to you, preferably one that is already funding your agency. Second, select one of your agency's programs or projects that best matches this funder's giving priorities. Third, write the opening paragraph of a cover letter to this funding source.

ACCOMPANYING DOCUMENTS

Like celebrities, the narrative proposal and cover letter rarely travel alone. They are usually accompanied by a retinue of supporting documents. I divide attachments into two camps: those that almost always will be included with the submitted proposal and those that will travel along only with certain submissions.

What circumstances dictate whether an attachment is mandatory or optional? If the funder requests that a document be attached, then it is mandatory. Otherwise, consider the following questions before enclosing anything in addition to the proposal narrative:

- Does the item advance or enhance the narrative story?
- Does the item make the case for support more persuasive?
- Does the item provide the grantmaker with crucial information that's not otherwise covered in the written proposal?

If your answer to any of these questions is a definite yes, then it's probably okay to include the material. But if you're not certain, I recommend leaving it out of the submission packet.

When contemplating what attachments to include, the rule is: less is more. Generally speaking, grantmakers don't want any more information than what they expressly request. Be assured that the merits of a grant proposal are measured not by pounds or inches but by the strength of the program. Loading up a submission with lots of filler material will not improve an ill-conceived idea or make a weak proposal any stronger. As a practical matter, funders don't have the storage space to keep all the extraneous material that comes in with a submitted proposal. In fact, it's likely that all this stuff will get tossed into the circular file. So why not save them the trouble by leaving out anything that's not absolutely relevant?

The following sections offer some recommendations concerning what's mandatory and what's not when it comes to attachments. Remember, the grantmaker always has the final say. If a funder asks for a specific attachment, even if it is one I haven't mentioned, be sure to send it along.

Mandatory Traveling Companions

The following documents almost always accompany the proposal narrative:

• *501(c)(3) letter (also known as the "IRS determination letter")*. This is an agency's proof that it has qualified for tax-exempt status under the rules and regulations of the Internal Revenue Service. Funders don't make grants to for-profit businesses; therefore it is essential for the grantmaker to know that your agency is a bona fide nonprofit organization. This letter provides that assurance.

• *Board of directors list*. Funders want to see the composition of your agency's governing board. A list of an agency's board of directors with their professional affiliations gives the funder important information about board size and composition. Much can be learned by examining a board list, such as whether the board members adequately represent the community being served by the agency, whether the board is diverse, and what kinds of people serve on the board.

• *Agency's annual budget*. If your proposal seeks funding for a specific program, then include a program budget, as discussed in Chapter Eight. In addition to a program budget, also include a copy of your agency's current annual budget. This is the umbrella budget that covers all agency operations. An agency budget gives the funder information about how large the agency is financially and shows whether the agency is projecting to break even, have a surplus, or operate in the red. If program funding is being sought, the overall budget also informs the funder about the program's fiscal scope in relation to other programs operated by the agency. If your request is for general operating or unrestricted support, you will need to submit only the agency's annual budget.

• *Financial statements*. Generally, grantmakers want to review an agency's most recent financial statements, though occasionally they will ask for financial statements for two or more prior years. Financial statements show past performance: how much revenue was raised and how much money was spent. They indicate whether an agency is operating in the black (a good sign) or with a deficit (a big red flag). Financial statements may be audited, reviewed, or unaudited.

Financial statements that have been examined by an outside accounting firm as part of a thorough audit of an agency's financial records are *audited* financial statements. At the conclusion of the audit, the accounting firm will issue an opinion letter, which will either give the agency a clean bill of financial health or set forth recommendations for how the agency can improve its bookkeeping, accounting, or money management practices. Because audits are expensive, most funders do not expect small-budget agencies to present audited financial statements. By "small-budget" agencies I mean those with annual budgets of about $300,000 or less. When an agency's annual budget starts approaching $300,000 or more, it is time to consider an annual audit. Many grantmakers have guidelines that specify the budget size of agencies it requires to submit audited financial statements.

Reviewed financial statements mean that the accounting firm has not conducted a thorough examination of the accounting books and records, but rather have taken some steps to review the records and procedures. In contrast, *unaudited* financials mean that the agency's financial information is presented "as is" and without the benefit of examination or review by an outside, independent accounting firm.

• *List of other funding sources for the program.* Grantmakers are always interested in knowing which other foundations, corporations, and government agencies have committed, or will be approached to commit, funds for the program they are being asked to support. I recommend that you include this list as a separate attachment rather than providing this information in the program budget (you'll recall that in the budget, revenue sources are only listed by category, such as "foundation grants"). The reason for keeping this list separate is that this information will need to be updated frequently as the agency submits proposals to new potential funders and as funding decisions are made. I suggest that you separate this list into three sections. In the first section, report all grantmakers that have committed funds so far. In the second section, list funders to whom proposals have been submitted and are currently pending. Finally, if the agency has identified other potential funding sources to whom it intends to submit proposals but hasn't yet done so (perhaps because a deadline is still several months off), then include a third section showing agencies to be applied to. Table 10.1 shows a sample of the format I use for the list of other funding sources.

Table 10.1
Sample List of Other Funding Sources

Funder by Grant Status	Amount of Grant (in Dollars)
Committed funds	
The Community Foundation	$30,000
The Jean Therrien Family Foundation	15,000
The Forrest Fund	10,000
Really Big Company	7,500
Pending proposals	
Local Government Agency	45,000
The Schwalbe Family Fund	10,000
Midsize Corporation	5,000
To be applied to	
International Company	10,000
Rasicot Foundation	20,000

Optional or Occasional Traveling Companions

The following are traveling companions that may accompany the narrative in certain cases:

• *Board of directors resolution.* Funders want evidence that an agency's governing body is aware of the activity for which funding is being sought and that they have approved of the agency's seeking grant support to fund this work. A board of directors resolution provides this evidence, and more and more funders are requesting it. This document, signed by the board secretary, attests to the fact that the board voted and approved of the submission of the proposal.

• *Brochures or newsletters.* Sure, brochures and newsletters look nice, they often cost a bundle to print, and your agency has ten cartons of them in storage. But is it necessary to include a brochure? Only if doing so will substantially augment your written narrative. For instance, if the brochure or newsletter contains photographs (sharp and in focus!) of the program in action—photos that visually illustrate your agency's story—then you might consider enclosing one with the proposal packet. Make sure that what you send is current. An old newsletter is outdated and irrelevant. Keep in mind that fancy four-color, high-gloss brochures may give the wrong impression of your agency. Unless the cost to produce the brochure has been underwritten and this is plainly stated on the brochure, the grantmaker may think that your agency spends too much money on marketing materials and not enough on its programs. For all these reasons, the answer to the question of whether or not to include a brochure or newsletter is not automatically yes.

• *Photographs.* The same considerations discussed with regard to brochures and newsletters apply to photographs. It's rare for a proposal packet to include photographs. I would include them only if they can somehow meaningfully illustrate or complement the written story. If photos are enclosed, make certain they are sharp and in focus. Fuzzy photos do little to advance your agency's case.

• *DVDs.* It is almost never a good idea to enclose a DVD. If a classy brochure seems costly, what will a funder think about a jazzy DVD? The one possible exception concerns funders of the arts, as they often ask performing groups to submit a short DVD of a performance along with the grant application.

• *Graphs and charts.* Graphs and charts often can convey information more effectively than words and pictures. For example, a rising bar graph instantly shows the reader that something is increasing. It is a visual snapshot of a situation. There may be good reasons to include these illustrative materials from time to time. Graphs and charts can be placed either at the end of the proposal with the other attachments or within the text of the proposal itself, though sometimes this can be technologically difficult with electronic submissions. I caution you not to overwhelm the reader with dozens of graphs and charts. The impact of one or two is usually more powerful than that of several.

• *Memorandum of understanding or collaboration agreement.* If your nonprofit agency is collaborating with another organization on the program for which you are seeking grant funding, then you should enclose a copy of the signed memorandum of understanding or collaboration agreement.

• *Résumés or curricula vitae.* It is sometimes appropriate to enclose the résumés or curricula vitae (the fancy name for résumé that is used in the academic field) for the key people who will manage or implement the program or project. Funders are interested in seeing the qualifications (educational background and work experience) of those who will be in charge of the program. Having qualified people helps ensure the program's success. Résumés are often essential in the education and health care fields, where accredited professionals are frequently required in order to perform certain duties.

• *Articles of incorporation or bylaws.* For the most part, these are boilerplate legal documents and are not necessary enclosures. Articles of incorporation substantiate that the nonprofit agency has been lawfully incorporated in the state where it "resides," which usually means where it is headquartered and conducts its business. The articles of incorporation also show the legal name of the agency. Bylaws are an internal agency document that sets forth the policies and procedures for the governance of the organization. Such issues as the number of directors and their term of office, as well as nomination and removal policies, are covered in agency bylaws.

• *Work plans or organizational charts.* Usually work plans are internal documents describing specific tasks, the persons responsible for completing the tasks, and task deadlines. Work plans are like blueprints for the successful implementation of the program or project. Organizational charts show the agency's management structure, the chain of command in an organization. Enclose a work plan or an organizational chart only if it is requested by the funder.

• *Table of contents.* If a proposal packet contains many pages of attachments (say twenty or more), then I suggest adding a table of contents to help the reader navigate through these accompanying documents. When the attachments are extremely lengthy, it is also okay to place a tab on each separate item, using a numbering or lettering system, which is then keyed to the table of contents.

DELIVERY OF THE PROPOSAL

Once the packaging of the proposal is complete, it must be delivered to the prospective funder. Always use the delivery method specified by the grantmaker. If the funder prefers an electronic submission, then submit online. If the funder prefers a hard-copy submission, you have a few options.

One option is to personally hand-deliver the proposal. Obviously, this is feasible only if the funder is close by. Even so, hand-delivering the proposal is really only necessary if you are squeezing the proposal in under a deadline. For most submissions, a more reasonable option is to mail your proposal through regular delivery using the U.S. Postal Service, which provides remarkably reliable service considering the daily volume of snail mail it handles. You must allow sufficient time for your proposal to get to its final destination, whether that is on the other side of town or across the continent. Therefore, it is in your agency's best interest not to be working on a submission at the eleventh hour.

If a proposal gets finished only a day or two before it's due, you are probably forced to use express mail, an overnight delivery service, or (the worst-case scenario) a courier service. However, these are not generally recommended options, for two reasons. First, they signal to the prospective grantmaker that your agency probably did not plan ahead and budget enough time to finish the proposal with much time to spare. Second, using an expensive delivery method such as these suggests to the funder that your nonprofit organization has "extra" money to spend, that it doesn't conserve its financial resources for truly important financial needs. Certainly, none of us who work in the nonprofit field want to give that impression!

Another option is to use certified mail so you'll be absolutely certain that the proposal arrived at its destination. Although this is reassuring to you, I don't recommend using certified mail. Many grantmakers, especially small family foundations, do not have full- or even part-time staff members, and this means that there may be no one in the office to accept and sign for a certified delivery. Instead, a trustee will have to go to the post office to pick up the proposal. This can be an inconvenience. First impressions count, and this is not likely to be the one you'll want your agency to make.

Faxing proposals is an alternative I don't recommend, even to those rare funders that accept faxed submissions. No matter how sophisticated the equipment, a faxed copy never looks as professional as a clean original, and faxed copies do not photocopy well.

REPACKAGING YOUR PROPOSAL: THE LETTER FORMAT

In Chapter Three, I discussed letters of inquiry, and in subsequent chapters, I described how to write a successful formal proposal. There is one additional type of written narrative in the grantwriting field: the letter proposal. A letter proposal presents your narrative story in a letter format. Letter proposals have always been favored by corporate grantmakers, no doubt because they mirror the business letter format. However, today the letter format is popular among both corporate and foundation grantmakers, so it is important that you be acquainted with it.

There are two major differences between a formal proposal and a letter proposal. First, a letter proposal is printed on agency letterhead, whereas a formal proposal is presented on plain, white bond paper. Accordingly, proper letter etiquette should be followed when drafting a letter proposal, and this means including the date, an address, a salutation, and a signature. In other words, a letter proposal is precisely that: a letter.

Second, a letter proposal is usually shorter than a formal proposal, though generally not as brief as a letter of inquiry. A typical letter proposal will run between three and five pages, although I have written a few letter proposals that have run as long as ten pages. As is true with formal proposals and letters of inquiry, you should always refer to a funder's specific guidelines to see if there are any restrictions on length. It is common for funders to state the following: "Submit your request in a brief letter." It's this emphasis on being brief that makes the letter proposal often somewhat shorter than a formal proposal.

How do you know what proposal format to use? Consult the funder's guidelines. Most grantmakers will state their preference, but in the absence of specific guidelines, I usually choose to use the formal proposal format.

Other than the two main differences just mentioned, a letter proposal is in every other way exactly the same as a formal proposal. All the elements you use to create a compelling and convincing proposal story are included in a letter proposal: a heroic agency, clients who are the main characters in your story, a problem or unmet need that must be addressed, a location where the story takes place, conflict and tension, and a realistic resolution to the problem through the services delivered by your agency. The letter proposal is a variation in the packaging of your agency's story. I provide two sample letter proposals in the Appendix.

SUMMARY

Completing a manuscript is only the first step in getting a book published and into the hands of readers. Similarly, writing the narrative story for a grant proposal is just one step in the grantseeking process. There are what seem like a million details to take care of before a proposal arrives in the funder's office.

Here are some of the key things to think about when getting your proposal ready for submission:

- When possible, try to determine the grantmaker's preference for receiving the proposal: electronic or hard copy.

- If you are submitting electronically, be aware of any space and formatting limitations.

- If using a hard-copy format, print your proposal in eleven- or twelve-point type on plain, white bond paper and use a giant paper clip rather than binders, folders, or staples.

- If using a hard-copy format, prepare a cover letter to accompany the proposal.

- Certain items, such as the agency's 501(c)(3) letter, board of directors list, and annual budget, are almost always attached with the proposal. Other items are attached only when the funder asks for them or when for some other good reason it is appropriate to do so.

- When submitting a hard copy, there are many delivery options, but regular mail is probably the best.

- A letter proposal contains all the elements of a formal proposal, except that it is presented in a letter format and is usually somewhat shorter in length.

Site Visits and Beyond

Interacting with Funders

If a written proposal is analogous to a novel, then a site visit is like a stage adaptation of the written narrative. In a site visit, your agency's written story comes alive. A site visit gives a program officer or other representative from the funder's office an opportunity to see firsthand the work being done by the agency and the clients being served, and to meet people associated with the agency. A site visit also enables the program officer to ask more detailed questions about your agency's request and to hear what your agency's team has to say.

HOW TO STAGE A SITE VISIT

For a nonprofit agency to orchestrate a successful, informative site visit, everyone participating must be fully prepared. Just as in a stage presentation, all the performers (in this case, participants) must have the same script, and each must fully understand the role he or she is expected to play. Most often, it is the fund development staff that orchestrates a successful site visit. Because your role is likely to be that of "director," here are a list of tips that will help you prepare for and execute a site visit that best showcases your agency.

• *Find out who your audience will be.* You need to know who is coming for the visit and whether your agency is hosting one program officer or an employee contributions committee of twelve. Find out as much as you can about the people you will be meeting. Foundation and corporate Web sites are an excellent source of information and frequently include bios, and occasionally even photos, of staff members.

• *Determine where you'll meet.* Program officers typically prefer to meet at a location where clients are being served rather than at an agency's administrative offices. This means that a site visit may occur at a school, in a performance hall, at a medical clinic, in a homeless shelter, and other places where agencies do their work. Be certain to make the appropriate arrangements with your agency's program staff well in advance so that they are prepared.

I know of one case involving a social service agency that runs a needle exchange program in the "skid row" neighborhood of a major U.S. city. The agency arranged for the program officer to meet with agency staff at midnight and to spend an hour with them walking the streets and conducting needle exchanges with IV drug users. No doubt, that experience was a real eye-opener—and made a considerable impression on the program officer—for the agency received the grant.

Another site visit had a less happy ending. This case involved a new and inexperienced executive director of a child development center. When a program officer called to arrange a site visit, the executive director replied, "Let's schedule your visit after 3:30 P.M. because that's when the children go home, and it will be much quieter." The executive director missed the point. By shielding the program officer from "real life" at the center, she lost an opportunity to showcase the outstanding work being done by her staff of professional child-care workers. No doubt there would have been countless photo-op moments, none of which can be duplicated in the executive director's office. Not surprisingly, this agency didn't get the requested funding.

• *Confirm, preferably in writing, the date and time of the site visit.*

• *Respect the amount of time your visitors have allocated for their visit, but also be flexible if your guests decide to extend their stay.* If your visitors indicate that they have forty-five minutes to spend at your agency, plan carefully to make the most of the allotted time. If at the end of the forty-five-minute period, your visitors say they can stay longer, by all means accommodate their request. Certainly, there's more you can show and tell.

• *Consider carefully which agency personnel should meet with the funder representatives.* Staff participants are likely to include your agency's executive director, development director or grantwriter (or both), and program director (if the grant request will support a specific program). In addition, you may want a board member and agency client also present.

Determine in advance what role will be played by each participant. For example, an executive director may talk about the agency's history, its present state, and the vision for the future. A program director can provide detailed information about the program. A board member can discuss the community's involvement and support, while a client can personally attest to the value of the provided services. Development staff can present information about funding sources and needs.

• *Brief each site visit participant about the grant request and why the funder representatives are visiting.* Provide each participant with a copy of the grant proposal and, because you cannot be certain every person will read it, hold individual or group meetings to go over the essential points in the proposal and rehearse what people will say.

The following story illustrates what can happen when people aren't adequately prepared. An agency was hosting a crucial site visit with a representative from the local community foundation. The agency wisely invited a board member to attend the site visit but failed to brief him about the specifics of the grant request. During the visit, the program officer asked a question about the program's objectives. The board member blurted out, "I'd like to know the answer to that question too. I've asked it at board meetings and still don't think I've gotten a satisfactory answer." Ouch! This comment not only embarrassed the agency's staff but also jeopardized the agency's chances of getting the grant.

• *Script the site visit.* Consider who will meet with the visitor, for how long, and what key points should be covered by each member of the agency team. Make certain that all team members understand their "assignments." Rehearse answers to frequently asked questions in advance.

• *Help the agency team understand that the information disseminated during a site visit does not need to be sugarcoated.* Program officers are generally well aware of the challenges and difficulties confronted by nonprofit agencies. Honest, straightforward answers are always appreciated.

• *Be prepared to conduct a little improvisational theater if necessary.* Anticipate that a question you haven't previously thought of will arise during the visit or that the schedule won't go quite as planned. If this happens, improvise!

• *Provide a map or directions to the place where people are to meet, especially if you are hosting out-of-town visitors.* A site visit really begins the minute your visitors leave their office, so help make it a smooth experience by giving clear, simple directions or perhaps even arranging transportation.

• *Provide coffee and other modest refreshments as appropriate.* Your agency does not need to arrange catering from a four-star restaurant, but coffee and rolls might be welcomed for early-morning meetings, and a simple box lunch could be offered when a site visit straddles the noon hour.

• *Be careful not to misinterpret a site visit.* Don't assume that a site visit means that the grantmaker is absolutely going to give your agency the grant. A site visit means that your agency's funding request has caught the attention of the program officer and that this person wants to learn more before making a funding decision.

Site visits help break down those imaginary barriers that too often exist between grantmakers and grantseekers. Staff members have an opportunity to meet the people who will be making the funding decision. They will see that these individuals ask thoughtful questions and are generally intelligent, well informed, and genuinely interested in the work your agency is doing. On the other side, funders have a chance to meet those individuals who are making a difference in our communities by delivering valuable services to people in need. They will see how nonprofit staff work creatively with scant resources to achieve often impressive results.

COMMUNICATING WITH FUNDERS

What happens during the period of time after a proposal has been submitted but before the funder has made its decision? During this time, which from the nonprofit's viewpoint may seem interminably long, there are some basic rules of etiquette that the agency should follow:

• *Remember that honesty is always the best policy.* Be forthright and candid in all communications with the grantmaker. It doesn't do a nonprofit agency any good to hide or obfuscate the truth. It's a small world, and the nonprofit universe is even smaller, so half-truths and exaggerations are likely to be found out eventually. If a foundation inquires about a sensitive issue (for example, high staff turnover or lower than expected program results), be candid in your agency's response. I'm not suggesting that nonprofit agencies should showcase their faults on a marquee surrounded by neon lights, but they should try not to bury or hide trouble spots. It is preferable for an agency to be honest and direct while simultaneously putting a positive spin on a delicate or difficult situation.

• *Return telephone calls, e-mails, and other correspondence promptly.* It is absolutely crucial for nonprofit agencies to be responsive when a grantmaker telephones, e-mails, sends a letter, or otherwise communicates with the agency. This is a common courtesy as well as a wise thing to do. Inevitably, you'll get that call requesting additional information, such as a more detailed budget, the week you are extremely busy—such as when you are overseeing your agency's annual fundraising event. Although you may be tempted to hold off on responding to this request until after the event, don't—unless you have the foundation's approval. A delay, even one of just a matter of days, could spell disaster for your pending proposal. Suppose the foundation's trustees were meeting to decide on your proposal during that time period. Wouldn't you want them to have the benefit of reviewing a more detailed budget before making their decision? Similarly, it's just good business sense to promptly return all phone calls and other correspondence. If necessary, carve out some time during each day to do just that.

• *Don't make a pest of yourself.* It can seem like an eternity when a proposal is pending—and sometimes it takes quite a while. The internal review process at a foundation or corporation can take anywhere from a couple of weeks (which is very rare) to three to six months (this is about normal) to as long as eighteen months (believe me, this happens!). You will be strongly tempted to call and check in with the funder—often. But don't. If the funder has indicated that you'll hear back by a certain date, then I advise you to just sit tight and be patient until after that date has come and gone. After that date has passed, it is perfectly acceptable to check in—once—to find out about the status of your proposal. If the funder hasn't provided you with a date when you can expect a response, then it's okay to call and ask when you can expect to hear from them. To call more frequently is just pestering the grantmaker, and that's something your agency does not want to do.

These basic rules apply not just when a proposal is pending but to all communications between a nonprofit agency and a funder. It's just good common sense to be courteous all the time.

WHAT TO DO WHEN THE FUNDER SAYS NO

Someday, probably when your agency is least expecting it, an envelope arrives bearing the return address of the grantmaker. The day of reckoning has come. Do you do what I do and hold the envelope up to a light bulb, trying to discern whether a check is tucked inside? Receiving an answer from a potential funder is a lot like hearing from the critics. If there's approval, you get the money. If the reviews are tepid or unfavorable, what you receive is a "thanks but no thanks" letter.

If your agency gets a rejection letter, what's the appropriate response? Because it's entirely possible that your agency may want to apply again to this grantmaker in the following year, you should view this as an opportunity to begin to establish a relationship with the funder. Accordingly, you may want to send the funder a letter to say "thank you" for reading and considering your agency's grant request. Though it isn't essential to do so, this is certainly a cordial way to get your agency's name in front of the funder one more time.

Also try to find out how your proposal narrative can be improved for future submissions. I'm not suggesting that you phone a program officer and ask, "What was wrong with our proposal?" Rather, seek constructive feedback by phrasing the question this way: "Do you have any suggestions on how we can improve our proposal?" This is possible if you are able to reach a program officer by telephone. Unfortunately, you may not be able to reach all funders. Some foundations, particularly those small family foundations that don't have a full-time staff, may not have the capacity to respond to such inquiries, and other funders may simply not return phone calls or e-mails.

If you have the good fortune to reach a program officer, be prepared for one of two responses. One is that the program officer won't have any constructive suggestions because your agency's proposal was already strong and persuasive, but funding was denied solely because there were just too many other good proposals on the table and not enough dollars to go around. Or you will be fortunate enough to get some very useful feedback that can be addressed in future submissions to other funders. For example, maybe you'll learn that the proposal's accompanying budget didn't appear realistic to the funder because it seemed to present a financial picture that was either too optimistic or too pessimistic. Or perhaps the objectives stated in your proposal didn't seem realistic to the program officer. Maybe the program officer will reveal that the need you described didn't sound like an urgent one. Take what you hear, decide whether the criticism is valid, and make any appropriate changes to the proposal before it goes out the door next time.

When you are declined for funding, it is often important to remind yourself that there are many factors outside your control that play into the decision-making process, that the decision is not personal, and that even strong proposals get denied from time to time.

WHAT TO DO WHEN THE FUNDER SAYS YES

Let's suppose that, to your great delight, you receive notification that your agency has received the grant. What do you do? Although it's tempting to pop a champagne cork, the first thing to do is for someone from your nonprofit agency, preferably the executive director (or alternatively, the development director or grantwriter), to call the funder to say thanks. You can never offer too many thank-yous. And what better time to do so than when you're holding a check in your hand? The enthusiasm and excitement you're feeling are bound to transmit over the wire.

The next action to take is to follow up with a written acknowledgment letter. It is absolutely essential for nonprofit agencies to send a timely thank-you letter to the funder, ideally within forty-eight hours. This letter should be signed by the nonprofit's board chair, the executive director, or both.

Certain grantmakers, most often government granting agencies, require recipient agencies to sign a contract that states the terms and conditions governing the grant. If this is the case, it is prudent for your agency to promptly review the governing document, have it signed by the appropriate person (typically the executive director), and return it to the funder as soon as possible. It is often possible to enclose this contract with the acknowledgment letter.

The final step is for your agency to consider how it will publicly acknowledge the funder (unless anonymity has been requested). Publish donor lists in your agency newsletter and annual report. Post a donor list or create a donor wall in a public space at your agency's office. Send out an e-mail notification, press release, or both. Encourage a corporate funder to publicize its donation in its in-house publication. These are all effective ways to share your good news.

Going a step further, I also recommend that whenever new grant funding arrives, you notify each and every funder where you have a proposal pending. "Yahoo! We got funded" is the message you want to give. I'd first call the program officer because this gives me an excellent opportunity to build a personal relationship and share good news. Second, I'd follow up my call with a letter so that there is written documentation. The reason you want to do this is simple: money comes to money. When other funders invest in your agency, this is a good sign that yours is a credible organization worthy of support. So don't hide your good news; publicize it!

BEYOND THE GRANT AWARD

Building and maintaining a relationship with a funder continues during the grant period. It is a truism in all fundraising activities, and especially in grant-seeking, that the most likely future donor is a current one. Nonprofit agencies should carefully nurture their relationships with those foundations, corporations, and government agencies already supporting the cause. This means that nonprofit agencies should do the following:

- *Respond promptly to funder requests for information or materials.*

- *Submit in a timely manner any progress reports due during the grant period.* For example, many funders require grantees to submit quarterly financial reports and annual narrative reports. In fact, some funders make these a condition for receiving further progress payments under the grant. That's why it's a good idea to be prompt. (A grants follow-up calendar can help keep your agency on track.)

- *Keep the funder informed of significant changes in the nonprofit agency (such as an executive director transition), in the funded program or project, or even in the field.* Depending on the grantmaker, this communication can be via letter, e-mail, or telephone. When in doubt, ask the funder which method is preferred.

- *Consider inviting the grantmaker to appropriate agency events, though keep in mind that most program officers are so busy that they are unable to attend every function they are invited to.* Still, it's important on certain occasions (for example, the celebration of your agency's fiftieth anniversary) at least to let the grantmaker know that an event is taking place.

Maintaining a relationship with a grantmaker should be approached with the same thoughtfulness and courtesy that you extend to any relationship based on trust. Respect and nurture that relationship, and the audience of potential funders will be there. Fail to do so, and your audience will soon disappear.

SUMMARY

Telling your story doesn't end with the submission of a proposal. Site visits provide another forum for you to present your case for support to a potential funder. Consider a site visit as a theater piece that blends adherence to a script with improvisation. This chapter also covered those other occasions when it is appropriate for a nonprofit agency to interact with a funder, such as during the review process, when the funding decision has been made (whether yes or no), and during the grant period. Here are the key points to remember:

- Think of a site visit as similar to the stage adaptation of your written proposal.

- Make certain everyone who will participate in a site visit is well prepared. Give them the "script" (your proposal) and rehearse.

- Remember that a site visit isn't a guarantee of funding.

- Be open and honest in all communications with funders.

- When a funder says no, try to find out how your proposal can be strengthened for future submissions.

- Thank funders that say yes and find appropriate ways to recognize their support.

Beyond Grants
Applying the Storytelling Method

chapter
TWELVE

Whether you're a one-person development shop juggling several different fundraising balls or someone who is currently a full-time grantwriter but likely to expand beyond proposal writing at some point in your career, the skills you've learned in this book can be applied to communications beyond the grant proposal. Storytelling has universal application to all types of nonprofit (and for-profit, for that matter) communications. From brochures to banquet speeches, you can use storytelling to communicate your agency's message more effectively. Let's look at some of the more common communications tools used today in the nonprofit world.

ELEVATOR SPEECH

An elevator speech is a brief pitch, sixty seconds or so, in which you verbally present your agency's case for support. You and all other ambassadors of your agency (namely, board members, volunteers, staff) need a succinct speech for those short encounters with someone who is unfamiliar with your agency. It doesn't matter whether these encounters take place in an actual elevator, at a cocktail party, or in an airport lounge. An elevator speech answers the questions, What does your agency do and Why is this important? Your response is a supercondensed version of your story. Recall Chapter Four's discussion on opening your proposal

169

story with a hook. Think about how a strong, snappy opening sentence applies when crafting your agency's elevator speech. If you can successfully condense your agency's longer story to a succinct sound bite of substance, you are likely to engage the listener. If successful in sparking the interest of the listener, you may be invited to provide more detail either in the moment or at a later date. This is the goal of an elevator speech.

MISSION STATEMENT

When put on paper, an elevator speech often makes a darn good mission statement. A mission statement informs an audience about the nature of your agency's work and motivates a response, which may be to donate funds or volunteer time. The best have a powerful emotional component. In the normal course of writing proposals, grantwriters frequently write or, more accurately, rewrite mission statements. I discussed mission statements in Chapter Four, commenting that too often mission statements are too long, lacking in energy, and uninspiring. They are frequently written by committee, which may explain why they have these common flaws. My advice is this: an agency should seek input from its key stakeholders—board members, staff, and volunteers—about the key concepts its mission statement should convey. Then turn over the actual wordsmithing to the agency's best writer. A skilled grantwriter is well suited to this task.

CASE STATEMENT

I see two types of case statements being used in the nonprofit community today. The first is an internal document (ranging from one to five pages in length) that summarizes your agency's mission, vision, core values, programs, staffing, and financial health. The purpose of the internal case statement is to give all the reasons why someone would want to support your agency. This document ensures internal agreement on key facts about the agency and provides a foundation when drafting other materials for external audiences, such as grant proposals, appeal letters, and the like. A colleague of mine astutely observed that a grant proposal for general operating support often serves as an agency's case statement. I agree with her. You can thus see the direct link between storytelling in a grant proposal and storytelling in an internal case statement.

The second type of case statement is used in capital and endowment campaigns to inspire potential donors, especially lead gift and major donors, to contribute to the campaign. I've seen capital campaign case statements range from simple one-pagers to multipage, color-photo-enhanced brochures. No matter how plain or fancy the presentation materials, the agency is striving to deliver a compelling, inspiring, and, more often than not, emotional case for support. The best capital campaign case statements tell a story, skillfully blending the necessary facts and figures (dollar goals, timeline, and so on) with highly descriptive words and phrases (think back to Chapter One's writing exercise that focused on adjectives and adverbs). Given the number of competing campaigns often occurring simultaneously in a community, effective campaign statements must also do a good job of presenting a compelling need (refer to Chapter Five).

APPEAL LETTERS

Appeal letters are probably the most obvious vehicle for applying the storytelling method. Typically, appeal letters have an emotional tone, as they are used to motivate individuals to make a donation, be it a first-time, renewal, or upgraded gift (it is rare for major gifts to come in response to a written appeal). An appeal letter must open with a strong hook. This encourages the reader to keep reading. Appeal letters use vivid, precise language. They frequently incorporate client stories and quotes (as discussed in Chapter Five). The need must be obvious and urgent. Like a grant proposal, an appeal letter is most often composed of several different components. At minimum, there's the outer envelope, a remit envelope or other remit device, and the letter itself. Especially with acquisition pieces, a token gift (address labels, a bookmark, plant seeds, and the like) might be enclosed. Each individual component in the package must complement the others, and the message in all components should be a consistent one. The goal of an appeal letter is to persuade and motivate the recipient to immediate action—writing a check! As you can see, there are many similarities between an appeal letter and a proposal. Given these similarities, it should be no surprise that outstanding grantwriters often write the strongest appeal letters.

BROCHURES

Before the Internet, a brochure was one of the agency's primary marketing tools. Though less glorified today, a brochure can still be an effective way to present information about a nonprofit agency. They fulfill a useful function because this is a physical document you can leave with or send to a potential funder. Brochures run the gamut from simple to sophisticated. In a brochure, the inclusion of photographs and graphics adds another dimension to the telling of your agency's story. This is one of the areas where a brochure departs from a grant proposal. As discussed in Chapter Ten, photographs and graphics are used sparingly in proposals, if at all. When included in a brochure, images should complement the words, and photos should be clear and in focus; fuzzy images don't do much to enhance your story. As is true with a grant proposal, a brochure has space limitations, and the writer must decide on what's important enough to include and then convey this information with an economy of words. For these reasons, proposal writing is excellent training for brochure copywriting and vice versa.

WEB SITE CONTENT

Your agency's Web site affords an amazing opportunity for potentially millions of people to learn about your agency. I think of a Web site as an electronic brochure. It should not only present information clearly and concisely and be easy to navigate but also tell your agency's story. Web sites can do this through a vibrant marriage of words, photographs, and graphics, as found in an effective hard-copy brochure. A Web site may include client anecdotes, quotes, and testimonials. Some even include streaming video and sound. Although the technology and format may be new and changing, the basics remain the same. So once again, you can see that the skills developed as a grantwriter are transferable to drafting Web site content.

ANNUAL REPORTS

Annual reports are the wrap that often surrounds an agency's financial statements. Like a warm wool coat on a cold day, this wrap can be both functional and stylish. The most important function for an annual report is to disclose the agency's financial health in the published financial statements. As discussed in Chapter Eight, financial statements report actual income and earnings for a particular time period, namely the agency's fiscal year (which may or may not coincide with the calendar year). Annual reports also frequently contain information about a nonprofit agency's current programs and describe the successes achieved in the previous year. They present another opportunity for conveying an agency's story. Like brochures and Web sites, annual reports use words, photographs, and graphics in delivering information. Like capital campaign statements, annual reports come in all shapes, sizes, and degrees of decorativeness. And like grant proposals, they tell a story. Who is better qualified to tell that story than someone who has learned the craft by writing proposals?

GOVERNMENT GRANTS AND STORYTELLING?

I now want to address the topic of government grants. Government granting agencies include those at the federal, state, county, and local levels. Does the storytelling approach I've described apply to the writing and preparation of government grants? Yes, it can. I acknowledge that government grant applications are a topic unto themselves. Government grant applications tend to be more complex, with more rigid requirements and space limitations than what one typically encounters from other grantmakers. The formatting is different. The budget section is often onerous. Questions on the application form can seem redundant. Government grant applications are also usually far longer than proposals to a foundation or corporation. However, within the confines of a government grant application, I believe that you can infuse some, though not all, of the storytelling techniques presented in this book.

Accurately describing your story's antagonist (the need or problem) and setting realistic goals and objectives are the two sections most applicable. Every request for funding is about filling a need, and the greater and more urgent the need, the more likely it is to be funded. In a government grant application, you will also be asked to demonstrate the credibility of your agency by describing its prior accomplishments and achievements, which is covered in Chapter Four. You'll need to discuss how you will assess the program's success, as well as plans for sustainability (future funding), topics presented in Chapter Seven. You'll also need to pay particular attention to the accompanying budget and, as I emphasize in Chapter Eight, make sure that the numbers are consistent with information contained in the narrative. Having the storytelling approach in mind when preparing these portions of the narrative will result in a stronger presentation of your case for support.

There are notable areas where a storytelling approach is not appropriate in a government grant application. First, the overall tone and voice are likely to be more formal in a government grant application than in a request to a foundation or corporation. Use "third person impersonal" rather than first person.

Second, client anecdotes and quotes are rarely, if ever, included. The application forms usually don't give you enough space to include "extra" information like this. Furthermore, the awarding of government grants is analytical and process-driven. Because this is the case, the emotional component found in anecdotes and client testimonials plays a much less significant role. Third, because government grant applications are more formal, you should generally avoid using creative, marketing-type headings, which I otherwise recommend in Chapter Nine.

At the risk of being repetitious, I want to say again that grantwriting is as much an art form as it is a science. Experience makes you a better grantwriter. Over time, you'll develop almost a "sixth sense" regarding what storytelling techniques are appropriate to use in a given situation. Nowhere is this more true than when working on government grant applications. There will be entire applications and questions on applications where you'll "just know" that adding a dose of creativity is appropriate. You will also encounter applications when it works to your advantage to "dial down" on the creative storytelling.

BEYOND NONPROFITS

Some folks in the nonprofit field view grantwriting as a technical skill. They are partially correct. Certain aspects of grantwriting require technical proficiency. Designing and drafting the goals and objectives section of a proposal narrative come to mind. In large measure, government grantseeking does too. Yet grantwriting is also an art, as I believe I have demonstrated throughout this book. If grantwriting were purely technical, then it might be difficult for a grantwriter in the nonprofit field to transfer his or her skills. But it is not, and the skills are readily transferable to other forms of fundraising and to jobs outside the nonprofit field.

When the economy weakens, we often see people from the for-profit sector seek opportunities in the nonprofit field. Some will find satisfying jobs and remain in the field for the rest of their careers. Others will be unhappy, returning to the for-profit sector as soon as they can. Many individuals will enter the nonprofit field fresh out of college and never leave. Others will later seek new challenges and transition to the for-profit world. No matter what the circumstances, those individuals who gain grantwriting experience during their time in the nonprofit sector will take marketable, transferable skills to their for-profit jobs.

People with persuasive writing skills, which grantwriters have, will be good at writing marketing and advertising copy. Former grantwriters excel at preparing business proposals. Because grantwriters develop a passion for using clear, precise language, many find a new home in technical writing. They also become journalists, novelists, speechwriters, and teachers. There are any number of fields where a grantwriter can succeed.

Time to Write!

This is the final writing exercise. I hope this book has kindled within you a passion for grantwriting. Here's a way to find out. I ask you to think of five to seven words that describe your response to the word "grantwriting." Here are mine:

- Challenging
- Creative
- Puzzle-solving
- Strategic
- Rewarding
- Storytelling

What are yours?

AFTERWORD

Write what you know" is the mantra of all writing instructors. Become familiar with your nonprofit agency, its programs, and the people it serves. Understand the reason why your agency exists—the community problem or unmet need it seeks to address. This knowledge forms the foundation for all successful grantseeking.

Writing instructors also tell would-be writers that in reality there are only a handful of basic plots at their disposal. There's man versus the natural world; the one that goes boy meets girl, boy loses girl, boy eventually wins girl back (or vice versa); the one about jealousy and its negative consequences; and the universal plotline involving ambition at any cost and what the price really is. You get my point. Perhaps you can think of a few others to add to my list, but when you come right down to it, there aren't too many story lines to choose from. What makes a basic story different is the way an author tells it. That's why *Romeo and Juliet* isn't the world's only love story.

Storytelling in the nonprofit field isn't any different. Each nonprofit agency draws on the same basic plotline: a certain segment of the population living in a given community has an unmet need, and the nonprofit agency responds to that need. Yet each agency "owns" the rest of the story—the way it fills in the details—and that's what makes each proposal narrative unique. No other nonprofit tells its story exactly the same way. Just as there is no generic form for writing a novel or creating a short story, there is truly no universal template for crafting your agency's story and writing a successful grant proposal. That would be inconsistent with the creative process.

My hope is that the material presented in this book will help you in fashioning your agency's own original tale. That you will now approach the grantseeking task with renewed passion, energy, and enthusiasm. That you will eagerly soak up information about your agency and the field in which it operates. That you will thoroughly and efficiently research potential grantmakers, using all available resources. That you will not be discouraged by those who profess that an agency must have an inside connection in order to get grant funding, because it simply isn't true. That you will use any linkages to funders your agency has in a strategic, respectful, and ethical manner. And finally, that you will write with great passion and persuasion.

The mantra of grantmakers is "Tell us your story." This book has given you the tools to do just that. It's time for you to put this method into practice. This is your final writing exercise: write a full narrative proposal for a program or project worthy of grant support. I wish you tremendous grantwriting success!

The Final Manuscript: Two Letter Proposal Samples

REQUEST FOR A PROGRAM TO ASSIST VISUALLY IMPAIRED OLDER ADULTS

Paige Bissinger
Program Officer
Many Bridges Foundation
P.O. Box 00011
Any City, NY 00011

Dear Ms. Bissinger:

It's hard for older adults to maintain their health if they cannot see well enough to read the labels on their medication or prepare meals safely or get themselves to medical appointments. Our Center gives blind older adults the tools and skills to meet these challenges and maintain their health and independence. We are grateful for the $5,000 grant from the Many Bridges Foundation received in February 2007 and ask that you consider a grant of $10,000 for our work this year.

Organizational Background and Mission

The Lions Center for the Visually Impaired of Diablo Valley is a 501(c)(3) non-profit organization with a service area covering all of Contra Costa County. We are the only agency in the county providing independent living skills training for the visually impaired adult community. The Center has played a key role in the county since 1954 and is certified by the California Department of Rehabilitation.

Our mission is to develop the self-confidence and abilities of blind and visually impaired adults in Contra Costa County and to act as a resource of information and expertise to the community. The Center provides services to people in their homes and also offers Center-based group activities. All services are provided free of charge to the clients.

Since many visual impairments are related to age, most of our clients are older and are often dealing with other chronic health problems. Elderly women are the fastest growing population of blind or visually impaired Americans. Thus, most of our clients are low-income women over age 65 who live alone. The 1,347 individuals we served in FY2005–06 reflect the following profile:

- 90% are low income, including 58% with annual incomes of less than $13,800 a year.

- Macular degeneration is the leading cause of blindness (44%). Other causes include cataracts, glaucoma, diabetic retinitis, and other chronic conditions.

- 78.5% are over the age of 65; 72.8% are women; 58% live alone.

- Ethnicity closely parallels the profile of older adults in Contra Costa County: Caucasian (74%), African American (4.5%), Hispanic (15.4%), Asian (3.2%), Native Hawaiian–Pacific Islander (1.2%), Other (1.7%).

Our Programs

Our *Senior Independent Living Program* provides one-on-one in-home assessment, orientation, and training to adults with vision impairments. Staff made 1,680 home visits last year to the clients described above to teach them how to shop and cook safely so they can maintain good nutrition; to train them to use white canes and public transit to cross streets and travel safely in their community; to teach them how to manage their medications even if they cannot see the labels; to give them instruction in adaptive living skills such as personal grooming, housekeeping, and financial management; and to link them to peer support groups and activities so they can maintain good mental and emotional health. All services are aimed at helping clients make the best possible adjustment to their vision loss so that they can continue to live safely in their own homes for as long as possible. Spanish-speaking staff ensure that services are culturally appropriate for those with limited English.

When people lose their vision they tend to stay at home where they feel safe. The idea of leaving home is very frightening, but social isolation and inactivity often lead to boredom and depression. In addition to home visits by our staff, we also regularly sponsor *Group Classes and Activities* in order to meet our clients' needs for recreation and socialization. This includes two adult day programs tailored for the visually impaired—one in Pittsburg, the other in Pleasant Hill—and other activities such as a computer class, bowling, and field trips to places like Reno, Oakland A's baseball games, nearby farms for fruit picking, picnics, county fairs, and fishing trips. Hundreds of visually impaired seniors participate every year. We make extensive use of volunteers for these activities and logged more than 15,000 volunteer hours in our last fiscal year.

Adjustment to blindness and low vision is emotionally difficult for most people. Our Center sponsors 10 **Support Groups** led by professionals (our own staff and volunteers) throughout the county to help clients share their personal fears, anger, and frustration and receive practical tips and support from their peers. In the last fiscal year, 630 clients participated in our Support Groups. Typical topics include: How can you deal with the stages of grief that accompany loss of vision? How can you continue to feel comfortable while eating in front of others? How do you deal with family members who won't let you do anything for yourself? How do you deal with peers who treat you like you have some dread disease?

Request to the Many Bridges Foundation

We expect the demand for the services we provide to grow as the population ages. At the same time, new technology makes it possible for those with visual impairments to lead active, independent lives. The services of the Lions Center for the Visually Impaired are aimed at helping elders with visual impairments maintain their independence and dignity and improve their physical and mental health. Our annual budget is less than $500,000, but our services are worth many times that amount in terms of preventing illness and injury to our clients.

In the face of cutbacks in state funding, we must count on support from the private sector to fulfill our mission. We are requesting $10,000 to be allocated to the professional staff (outreach/vision specialists, rehabilitation teachers, orientation and mobility specialists) who provide services to our clients. If you have questions, need additional information, or wish to schedule a visit, please leave a message for me at the Center. I look forward to hearing from you.

Sincerely,

Walter Griffin
Board President and Acting Executive Director

Note: This letter proposal was written by fundraising consultant Susan Fox, coauthor of *Grant Proposal Makeover: Transform Your Request from No to Yes.*

REQUEST FOR A PROGRAM TO SUPPORT SCHOOL READINESS

Marcus Franklin
Executive Vice President
Worldwide Community Bank Foundation

Dear Mr. Franklin:

Living in the shadows of Marin County's affluence are thousands of poor and economically disadvantaged families. One of NBCC's core values is to serve this too-often hidden population.

On behalf of the low-income children and families served by the North Bay Children's Center (NBCC), I write this letter to the Worldwide Community Bank Foundation to request a grant of $7,500 for our school readiness and family literacy program.

NBCC is a 501(c)(3) nonprofit organization founded in 1986. Our mission is to provide the highest quality of child care at affordable levels to families across the income spectrum, as well as support services that nurture and enhance family life. For our first 10 years, NBCC operated in a 2700 sq. foot facility serving 60 children from birth through five years old. In 1996, NBCC became the first nonprofit organization to relocate to the decommissioned Hamilton Air Force Base as part of the base conversion project from military to civilian use. This new facility was larger, enabling us to better meet the growing child-care needs of our community by serving more families. During our 22-year history, we have served 1,350 children and families. We specifically reach out to low-income families, providing them with financial assistance and support services. These services include parent education and support programs, daily hot meals for the children, and scholarships for low-income families. More than 50% of the children served at NBCC receive tuition assistance, enabling parents to remain in or return to the workforce or continue their education.

Over the years, NBCC has had strong, long-standing relationships with other county and nonprofit agencies within our community. We work closely with Marin County's Health and Human Services Department, the Marin County Office of Education, and the Parents Service Project, an agency that helps develop family leadership. We also work with Easter Seals, Matrix, Catholic Charities, and

Novato Human Needs, and retain an early childhood mental health consultant from the Parents Place, a division of Jewish Family and Children's Service.

Last year, NBCC expanded its services to Sonoma County when the Petaluma City School District invited us to provide before- and after-school care and pre-school care at two elementary schools, one of which serves a predominantly low-income Latino/Hispanic population. With this expansion, NBCC serves more than 200 children annually: 150 children in Novato and 50 children in Petaluma.

NBCC is governed by a 15-member board of directors that includes members of the local business community, parents, and educators. Our 2007–2008 budget is $2,040,000, with approximately 13% ($270,000) raised from foundation and corporate grants and individual donations.

At our Novato location, we have 25 preschool children and their families participating in a school readiness and family literacy program. Activities are designed to increase reading and writing in the home and to prepare preschool-ers for a successful transition to kindergarten. All participating families are low-income and receive government subsidy. They are also all Latino, with English not being their primary language. The goal of this program is for us to fully inte-grate early childhood education with culturally appropriate parent support and adult education. First, we evaluate each participating family's individual literacy needs. Working together, NBCC staff and the participating parents then create a mutually agreed-on plan for the family. Plans may include parent enrollment in ESL classes, family participation in our "Raising a Reader" program (which gets culturally and linguistically appropriate books into the homes of low-income families), and parent attendance at NBCC-sponsored parent workshops and social gatherings. After an initial orientation meeting, NBCC staff meets with families periodically throughout the year to assess how the family plan is work-ing and to discuss their child's progress.

NBCC uses *The Creative Curriculum for Preschool,* which is a scientifically based, research-tested, comprehensive curriculum model that links curriculum to assessment and to content-area standards. The assessments are conducted for each child twice a year. Our goal is for each child to demonstrate an increase in con-tent knowledge across all curriculum areas. These areas of development include social-emotional, cognitive, language, physical, and nutrition education. Last year, every child who "graduated" from this program was eager and well prepared for kindergarten. In addition, parents left the program more knowledgeable and confident about their role as full participants in their children's education.

Our school readiness and family literacy program was launched in 2006 with seed funding from First Five Marin (a one-time grant) and the California Department of Education. This year, the program's budget is $81,332, which includes funding for a part-time bilingual teacher (for nine months during the school year), four staff training sessions focusing on cultural competency and early literacy, and three parent education evenings. Government contracts and subsidies cover only a portion of these expenses. So far, NBCC has raised $42,332 from state contracts and $3,000 from individual contributions. We have identified other potential grant funders and are in the process of submitting requests.

We respectfully ask the Worldwide Community Bank Foundation for a grant of $7,500. These funds will greatly assist us in serving low-income Latino children and families who live in Marin County. An effective school readiness and family literacy program helps lay the foundation for school success and ultimately success in life, so that these young children have a chance to move from the shadows of poverty to lives of economic stability and opportunity.

Thank you very much for considering our request. If you need additional information or have any questions, please feel free to contact me.

Sincerely,

Susan Gilmore
Executive Director

Encls.

INDEX

C

Calendars: grants, 31, 32; grants follow-up, 166
Capacity building funds, 10
Capital purchase funds, 10
Case statements, 170–171
Cash flow analysis, 124, 126–127, 128–129
Characters: introducing, 51–53, 55–56, 57–58; nonhumans as, 58; quoting, 13, 81–82; as story element, 3
Charts, 154, 155
Child advocate program, 71, 93
Child care centers, 74, 160
Citing sources, 48, 76
Clients: anecdotes about, 77, 80–81, 174; interviewing, 6, 12–13; introducing, 50, 57–58; needs of, 83; quotes from, 13, 81–82
Climactic moment, 3, 66. *See also* Goals and objectives section
Collaborations, 75, 154
"College Connect" program, 137
Communicating with grantmakers: after decision made, 164–166; after submitting proposal, 163; before preparing proposal, 30, 31–32; while proposal is pending, 162–163
Conflict. *See* Tension
Contact information: in cover letter, 146, 147–148; in letter of inquiry, 41
Continuing programs, budget for, 116–117
Corporate grantmakers, 17–18, 20, 60, 156–157
Costs: administrative, 121–123; evaluation, 103; overhead, 121–123. *See also* Budget
Cover letters, 146–150; content of, 33, 147–148; and electronic submissions, 143; letterhead for, 146–147; sample, 148–149; writing exercise on, 150

Credibility: and deficits, 21–22; establishing, for start-up agency, 54; establishing, in letter of inquiry, 41; of quotes, 48; and readiness for grantseeking, 9; from support of other grantmakers, 39
Curricula vitae, 154–155

D

Data, in needs statement, 75–77, 78–79
Deficits, 21–22, 127
Delivering proposals, 155–156
"Dirty draft," 14
Donors: publicly acknowledging, 165; researching, 27–28
DVDs, as attachments, 154

E

E-mail, 163
Early child development program, 104
Editing, 14
Electronic submissions, 30, 139, 142–144, 158
Elevator speeches, 169–170
Endowment funds, as financial need, 10
Environmental education programs, 44–45, 58, 105, 137
Epilogue, 101–106; content of, 103–104; how to write, 104; importance of, 101–102; sample, 104–105; summary of, 110–111; writing exercise for, 106
Equipment purchase funds, 10, 42–43
Established agencies, 25, 30, 53
Evaluation: cost of, 103; planning for, 102; reports after, 103–104; tools for, 102–103
Evaluation section. *See* Epilogue
Executive director: as contact person, 148; funding salary of, 121–122; interviewing, 12; signature of, 41, 148, 165; and site visit, 161–162; as source of ideas, 5; transition of, 9, 166

Expenses. *See* Costs

Expertise, and fundability, 6, 7

F

Fables, 1

Facts, caution on exaggerating, 77

Faith-based volunteer program, 40

Faxing proposals, 156

Field research, 6, 11

Financial needs: of agency's clients, 83; clarifying, 9–11; and identifying potential grantmakers, 21–22; types of, 9–10. *See also* Needs statement

Financial statements, 127, 143, 151–152

Fit: letters of inquiry demonstrating, 38–39, 40; method for determining, 18–24

501(c)(3) letters, 143, 151

Food bank, 84–85

Footnotes, 76, 118, 126

Format: for cover letter, 146–148; of electronic submissions, 30, 143; of goals and objectives section, 92; for government grant applications, 173; for list of other funding sources, 153; of methods section, 96–97; of paper submissions, 30, 144–146

Foundation Center, 26, 27

Foundations, 17. *See also* Grantmakers

Four-filter-plus-one method, 18–24

Fundability, determining, 6–7

Funders. *See* Grantmakers

Funding: attaching list of sources of, 152–153; strategies for, 108

Furniture recycling agency, 72, 82, 98, 110

Future funding section. *See* Sequel

G

General operating funds, 10, 114, 151

Geographic preference, of grantmakers, 18, 19–21, 60

Goals, 88–89

Goals and objectives section, 87–92; format of, 92; goals in, 88–89; and government grant applications, 173; length of, 92; objectives in, 89–92; overview of, 87–88; sample, 93, 94, 95; summary of, 99; writing exercise for, 95

Government grants, 18, 123, 173–174

Grant amount: deciding on, to request, 24–25; range of, as screening criterion, 22–23; requesting, in cover letter, 147; requesting, in letter of inquiry, 39

Grant applications. *See* Proposals

Grant proposals. *See* Proposals

Grant range. *See* Grant amount

Grantmakers, 17–35; advantages of letters of inquiry for, 37–38; communicating with, 30, 31–32, 162–163, 164–166; filter method for screening, 18–24; geographic preference of, 18, 19–21, 60; grant range of, 22–23; guidelines of, 30–31, 144–146, 157; IRS Form 990 for, 31; list of potential, 29–30; number of potential, 17–18, 25–26, 29–30; relationships between nonprofits and, 23–24, 33–34, 166; reports to, at end of funding period, 103–104; researching, 26–29, 34–35; responding to decision of, 164–166; screening procedure of, 132–133, 134–135; site visits by, 159–162, 167; subject area of, 19; and type of financial needs, 21–22

Grants: amount of requested, 24–25; government, 173–174; ratio of awarded, to submitted proposals, 8, 132; renewal of, 107; size of, given by grantmakers, 22–23

Grants calendars, 31, 32, 166

Grants follow-up calendar, 166

P

Packaging: of electronic submissions, 30, 143; of paper submissions, 30, 144–146

Paper: for cover letter, 146–147; for formal proposal, 144–145; for letter proposal, 157

Paper clips, 146

Parables, 1

Pascal, Blaise, 37

Personal connections, 23–24, 33–34

Petaluma Bounty, 84–85

Philanthropy By Design (PBD), 72, 82, 98, 110

Phone calls: after proposal rejected, 164; after receiving grant award, 165–166; after submitting proposal, 163; before preparing proposal, 30, 31–32

Photocopies, single- vs. double-sided, 145–146

Photographs, 154, 172

Pipher, Mary, 49

Place, creating sense of, 60–62

Planned Parenthood, 78

Planning: cash flow analysis for, 124, 126–127, 128–129; evaluation, 102; financial and cash flow, 59–60; for future funding, 107

Plot, 3, 65, 131, 177

Preparation: of budget, 113–114; for grantseeking, 5–13, 16; for grantwriting, 11–13, 16; for site visits, 159–162

Prison reform program, 81

Problem statement. *See* Needs statement

Program description. *See* Methods section

Program director, 5, 6, 12

Program officers, 33–34, 134–135

Programs/projects: defined, 9–10; determining fundability of, 6–7; letter of inquiry (LOI) for support for, 44–45; site visits to, 159–162, 167; support

for, as financial need, 9–10; titles of, 135, 137–138, 140. *See also* Budget, program

Proposal narrative, 47–111; antagonists in, 66–67; attachments to, 150–155; building tension in, 83, 85; citing sources in, 48, 76; elements of, 3; epilogue of, 101–106, 110–111; exaggerating facts in, 77; footnotes in, 76; goals and objectives section of, 87–92, 93, 94, 95, 99, 173; graphs or charts in, 154; introductory section of, 47–63; length of, 47; methods section of, 92–99; needs statement in, 67–85, 173; section headings in, 135, 138–140; sequel of, 106–111; uniqueness of, 177–178. *See also* Proposals

Proposals: bad/good classification of, 7–8; delivering, 155–156; first draft of, 13–14; for government grants, 173–174; individualizing, for different grantmakers, 142; letter, 156–157, 158, 179–184; packaging, 30, 144–146; preparation for drafting, 5–13, 16; ratio of reviewed vs. funded, 8, 132; reasons for using storytelling in, 2; responding to grantmaker's decision on, 164–166; review time for, 60, 163; summary of, 131–134, 136, 140; time required for writing, 14, 16. *See also* Attachments; Proposal narrative; Submitting proposals

Publications, information on potential grantmakers in, 28

Q

Quotes, 13, 48, 81–82

R

Relationships, between nonprofits and grantmakers, 23–24, 33–34, 166

Grant Proposal Makeover
Transform Your Request from No to Yes

Cheryl A. Clarke • Susan P. Fox

ISBN 978-0-7879-8055-9 • Paperback
Available wherever books are sold
www.josseybass.com

"Grantwriters, development directors, executive directors—all nonprofit executives who want to write high-quality grant proposals that catch and then keep the attention of donors should read this excellent guide."
—**Tony Silard, executive director, The Center for Social Leadership**

"Working through six major problem areas with examples plus invaluable comments by foundation staff, Clarke and Fox go far beyond the basic 'how-to-write-grants' book."
—**Michael Wells, CFRE and editor, *Charity Channel and Foundation Review*; author, *Grantwriting Beyond the Basics***

"This is one of the best tools for grantseekers I've seen in a long time."
—**Stephanie Roth, editor, *Grassroots Fundraising Journal*, Oakland, California**

Nine out of ten grant proposals are rejected. *Grant Proposal Makeover* shows how to transform lackluster proposals into excellent ones–that have the potential to be funded. This book stands out from other traditional grantwriting books because it illustrates common flaws and problems in proposals and shows exactly how to fix them. It also includes helpful tips and quotes from foundation program officers and funding community insiders taken from an international survey of foundation professionals.

Grant Proposal Makeover addresses common problems in proposals such as:

- Florid writing
- Too much detail
- Not enough detail
- Inordinant numbers of statistics
- Nondisclosure of the need
- Disorganization
- Split personality "Frankenstein" writers' voices

The book also addresses consistency, format, and side issues every proposal writer should think about before submission.

JOSSEY-BASS™
An Imprint of **WILEY**
Now you know.